"This is the most irresistible book I've read in a long time. Whether you use it to break out of a block, strengthen your writing muscles, or just have fun, it's guaranteed to spark your creativity and bring joy back to your writing process. A perfect gift for writer-friends, too!"

—JENNA GLATZER, EDITOR-IN-CHIEF, ABSOLUTEWRITE.COM, AND AUTHOR, *OUTWITTING WRITER'S BLOCK AND OTHER PROBLEMS OF THE PEN*

"Put this book on your *desk*—not in your bookcase—because you're going to want to refer to it every day! *The Write-Brain Workbook* is a perfect blend of writing prompts and take-it-to-the-keyboard action."

—MELANIE RIGNEY, FORMER EDITOR, WRITER'S DIGEST

"Normally I don't get excited about 'writing exercises'—possibly because they all start to look the same. That was, until I looked at Bonnie Neubauer's book—and thought, 'Hey, these look like FUN!' It's impossible to flip through the pages of this book without getting drawn in—and once you get hooked, you'll want to keep going. Plus, the applications at the bottom of each page definitely hit home; would I have ever realized that I sometimes play 'wicked stepmother' to my writing? This book is perfect for anyone who needs t jumpstart—or restart—their writing spark."

—MOIRA ALLEN, EDITOR, WRITING-WORLD.COM, AND AUTHOR, *STARTING YOUR CAREER AS A FREELANCE WRIT*

D0971380

"When I first saw Bonnie Neubauer's *The Write-Brain Workbook*, the first thing I did was ... start doing the exercises. I couldn't stop. I became an addict. I don't know a higher compliment for such a book. Her exercises were fun (not frivolous), educational (not busywork), creative (not rote), and pointed (not gratuitous). Each one singled out a particular aspect of writing and said, in the most encouraging, arm-around-the-shoulders way, 'Let's work on this.' I especially enjoyed the *Take the Next Step* boxes. Too many writing exercises stop dead once the exercise is over. Bonnie

Neubauer keeps connecting exercise to exercise, keeps the ripples expanding, the resonances ringing. She keeps reminding writers that what they do outside of the writing task (going to mentors for advice; thinking about writing when they're not writing; paying passionate attention to their individual writing process) cycles back into their work. Just like physical exercises, Bonnie Neubauer's compositional calisthenics clear the mind, tone the muscles, and get the heart going. *The Write-Brain Workbook* would make a great addition to many kinds of writing courses, from introductory composition to creative writing to nonfiction across the curriculum. Have to finish this blurb now and get back to those exercises...."

—JOHN TIMPANE, EDITOR, COMMENTARY PAGE,
PHILADELPHIA INQUIRER, AND AUTHOR, *POETRY
FOR DUMMIES*

"If you have trouble getting started with writing a chapter or a book, then you need to get *The Write-Brain Workbook*. The exercises in this book will get your creative fires burning and knock your writer's block off its block."

—JOHN KREMER, AUTHOR, *1001 WAYS TO MARKET
YOUR BOOKS*

"Ever have trouble getting started writing? No more. Just pick up a copy of *The Write-Brain Workbook*—Bonnie Neubauer's new book—and free the writer within you. These creative out-of-the-box daily exercises will help you to start fast and to keep on writing. Don't miss this one."

—BUD GARDNER, CO-AUTHOR, *CHICKEN SOUP FOR THE
WRITER'S SOUL*, AND AUTHOR, *OUTWITTING WRITER'S
BLOCK AND OTHER PROBLEMS OF THE PEN*

THE WRITE-
BRAIN
WORKBOOK

2007

Write on!

THE WRITE-BRAIN

BRAIN

WORKBOOK

• bonnie neubauer •

366
EXERCISES
to **liberate** your writing

WRITER'S DIGEST BOOKS
Cincinnati, Ohio
www.writersdigest.com

Photo by Anne Knoll,
www.knollphotos.com

BONNIE NEUBAUER is a late bloomer who didn't discover her creativity until she was in her thirties. Now in her late forties, her inventive energy enables her to continue to be a kid at heart, leaving creative sparks wherever she goes. In 1997, Bonnie met her husband-to-be in a writing group. In 2000 they got married at the same Borders store where they met. Although they lust after living full-time in an RV, they currently live in a crowded apartment in suburban Philadelphia with their two cats and all of Bonnie's stuff that she just can't seem to throw away. To enjoy more of Bonnie's creations, including Story Spinner, a round writer's wheel that generates millions of creative writing exercises, visit www.bonnieneubauer.com.

THE WRITE-BRAIN WORKBOOK. Copyright © 2006 by Bonnie Neubauer. Manufactured in China. All rights reserved. No other part of this book may be reproduced in any form or by any electronic or mechanical means including information storage and retrieval systems without permission in writing from the publisher, except by a reviewer, who may quote brief passages in a review. Published by Writer's Digest Books, an imprint of F+W Publications, Inc., 4700 East Galbraith Road, Cincinnati, Ohio 45236. (800) 289-0963. First edition.

Visit our Web site at www.writersdigest.com for information on more resources for writers.

To receive a free weekly e-mail newsletter delivering tips and update about writing and about Writer's Digest products, register directly at our Web site at http://newsletters.fwpublications.com.

10 09 08 07 06   5 4 3 2 1

ISBN 1-58297-355-5 (pbk.: alk. paper)

Distributed in Canada by Fraser Direct, 100 Armstrong Avenue, Georgetown, ON, Canada L7G 5S4, Tel: (905) 877-4411. Distributed in the U.K. and Europe by David & Charles, Brunel House, Newton Abbot, Devon, TQ12 4PU, England, Tel: (+44) 1626 323200, Fax: (+44) 1626 323319, Email: mail@davidandcharles.co.uk. Distributed in Australia by Capricorn Link, P.O. Box 704, S. Windsor NSW, 2756 Australia, Tel: (02) 4577-3555.

Edited by: Amy Schell
Cover design by: Claudean Wheeler
Interior design by: various (see pages 368-370)
Design coordinated by: Grace Ring
Production coordinated by: Robin Richie
Photography on pages 8, 17, 47, 95, 108, 112, 113, 132, 137, 160, 196, 200, 230, 285: Christine Polomsky

fw

F·W PUBLICATIONS, INC.

FROM THE AUTHOR

I am blessed to have so many wonderful and supportive people in my life. This thank you list merely reflects the top of the heap: Jennifer DeChiara for believing in my vision and running straight to Writer's Digest with it. Jane Friedman, Amy Schell, Claudean Wheeler, Grace Ring, and all the designers who took part in this book, for countless hours of alchemy that turned my pages of type into a beautiful book. Gildie Stein for his heart of gold and being the world's most loving, supportive, and funny husband. Mom and John, Dad and Rhoda, for teaching that love is always the right choice. Hope and Kim, sisters who know the real Bonnie and still stand by me through thick and thin. Alex, Tyler, Adam, and Josh for being the best nephews an aunt could ask for— and for sometimes letting me win at the games we play! Aunt Judi and Uncle Dave for loving me and bailing me out more than once. My grandparents who continue to watch over me. Ellen Fisher for the $1,000 check challenge, being my best friend, and catering to my picky eating. All my A.C.N. friends for the safest space imaginable, extraordinary coaching, and a huge pile of love notes. Rachel Simon for being a mentor, friend, and co-conspirator. Jennifer Hoff for picking me up—literally. Tom McDonnell for seeing my potential way before I did. Randy Rosler for igniting my creative spark and buying my first writing. Morgan Henderson for handing me my first gig. Borders and Barnes & Noble stores in the Metro Philly area for being the best places to grow, learn, and write. Borders Rosemont and Chestnut Hill writing groups for being willing (and amazingly able) guinea pigs. Carol Wicks for always being ready to create with me. Borders Springfield Pen In Hand Group for getting me started on the book writing path and especially Joe Donlan, for inviting Gil to attend. John Harnish for opening doors and making great introductions. Melanie Rigney for linking me into her chain of contacts. Women's Yellow Pages for being a great day job, complete with Babe and Caesar who always listen. Glenys Gustin for weaving a dream-come-true Web site. Allan Sherman for being my #1 creative influence. Booger (Bugaboo) and Coolio (Cookachoo) for making me laugh even when I'm cleaning their litter box.

DEDICATED TO MY MOM AND DAD, SANDY AND ARNOLD, WHO CONSISTENTLY PROVE THAT WITH LOVE IN YOUR HEART YOU WILL ALWAYS HAVE THE PASSION TO BEGIN AGAIN. AND TO GIL, THE LOVE OF MY LIFE.

BY RACHEL SIMON

FORE

Few silences prompt as much grief as the silence of a writer not writing. Whether caused by the beginner's fear of starting, the student's insecurity about continuing, or the author's despair over topping recent success, writers sometimes can't write.

It is for these people, the not-writing writers, that Bonnie Neubauer wrote *The Write-Brain Workbook*, a treasure chest of playful, get-going ideas, the kind every not-writer inevitably yearns to see.

I myself searched in vain for such a book seven years after my bleakest not-writing phase began when I was eighteen. Before that age, I'd written cartons of novels, stories, plays, and poetry. But then, perched on the end of my write-whatever-I-want childhood and the beginning of my aim-for-high-standards college years, my creativity froze. I had ideas occasionally, but I was so daunted by the enormous chasm between the way I'd always written and the way I hoped to write, that I couldn't bear the thought of putting pen to paper. Conveniently, the demands of my undergraduate education were formidable; I'll get back to writing, I told myself, after I finish this paper, this semester, this degree. By the time I'd lost the excuse of time, I was in my early twenties, working at such meaningless jobs that I acquired the new excuse of existential gloom.

Not until my mid-twenties did I get a decent job, and hence get serious about resuming. To do this, I determined, I would go to the library every day when I finished work at 5:00, and write in a carrel until I left for home at 9:00. Since I had not-written for so many years, I decided to begin every session by doing writing exercises. If one bloomed into something more substantial, so much the better, but if not, writing exercises would carry me through my allotted time every evening.

With this daily schedule in mind, I hurried to the bookstore, searched for a collection of exercises—and discovered, to my dismay and disbelief, that there were none to be had. In desperation, I bought some grammar books, and for the entire summer of my twenty-fifth year, I worked four hours a day on what amounted to eat-your-spinach exercises. Eventually, in the fall, I graduated to writing stories, and finally, after seven years, my writer's block came to an end.

WORD

Twenty years later, I met the exuberant writer Bonnie Neubauer, and learned about the existence, then only in manuscript form, of *The Write-Brain Workbook*. I knew before I had even seen a page that this was the book I'd searched for in my not-writing days, and, moreover, the book that would have spurred—rather than quenched—the enthusiasm of the many not-writers who'd sought my advice ever since. This is a book that promises not only a fresh exercise every day, but an exercise written in a spirit of fun. Bonnie sent me a copy, and I quickly incorporated it into my daily routine. Here I'd been recommending writer medicine for so many years. Finally I could recommend candy.

So now, every morning, I enjoy another page of *The Write-Brain Workbook*. What a treat it's been for me, and I hope will be for you. May a page a day drop the *not* from your identity, and make you the real writing writer you've always dreamed you could be.

—RACHEL SIMON, AUTHOR, *RIDING THE BUS WITH MY SISTER* AND *AUTHOR'S SURVIVAL GUIDE*

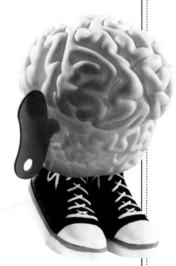

HOW TO USE THIS BOOK

The Write-Brain Workbook is designed to get you writing and keep you writing. Unlike other creative writing books, you will not be spending your time *reading* about writing. Instead, you jump in and immediately write—right in the book. All you need is a pen and ten minutes a day to enjoy this at-home workshop in workbook format. Always keep extra paper handy for those exercises that require it. At the end of the year you will have written at least 365 pages. That's quite an accomplishment. And not once during the year will you have faced a blank page. Every exercise gives you a starting phrase, an ending sentence, a series of challenging words to incorporate, a fill-in-the-blanks character to create ... and so much more. Many of the exercises are just like word games—totally fun!

AS PROMISED, THERE'S NO NEED TO READ FURTHER. OPEN TO ANY PAGE ... AND START WRITING! IF YOU PREFER TO KEEP READING, PLEASE DO.

This book is for novices who have always thought they'd like to write, as well as for experienced writers looking to try their hand at creative writing. The exercises are especially beneficial if you happen to be experiencing writer's block because they prompt you to write about out-of-the box topics without any expectations whatsoever. They are also fantastic warm-ups before settling down to your "real" writing. For those of you who keep journals, many of the exercises use personal experience as a jumping block. If you are a creative writing workshop junkie, you'll no longer have to wait until the next workshop. You now have one a day. Do them alone, at home, on vacation, or even create your own writing group and do them with your friends. You'll be amazed how unique each person's writing voice is.

With a little editing and polishing, you can turn many of the results of these exercises into stories, poems, articles, or even novels to be submitted for publication.

Your goal is to do one page a day. You are building momentum, a writer's best friend, by writing every day. Think of it as practicing your scales. (But these scales aren't repetitive or boring. They are more like being part of an improvisational jazz jam.)

The more you write, the better you write. So stick with it and watch yourself improve while you are having fun!

At the bottom of each page is a bonus one-minute exercise titled, **TAKE THE NEXT STEP**. These exercises will help you learn about your writing practice preferences. They will also assist you as you explore your personal writing process. These simple lessons can be applied immediately to your other writing.

Some basic rules to keep in mind while you are writing (or to rebel against if that's more to your liking):

KEEP WRITING: Don't stop. If you hit a block, write the last word over and over until something new starts flowing from your pen. Usually it's the word "and." Write "and and and and and and and and" and soon you will be writing "and I am sick of writing the word and. I am also sick of …" and you're off and writing again!

DON'T EDIT: Editing is left-brained work, and these exercises are right-brained fun. So don't go back and cross out or change words. Keep moving forward. And don't worry about spelling or grammar. There's plenty of time for that later. Just make sure you can read it!

LET YOURSELF GO: Don't worry about the end result. Give yourself permission to write junk. Don't hold back. Don't filter. Go on an adventure. Play.

BE SPECIFIC: Use all your senses to describe things. Use your sense of smell to describe a cab, your sense of taste to describe a computer. The best way for readers to recall what you've written is to be specific: Not "toy", but "plastic Batman figure missing an arm."

DON'T NEGATE YOUR WORK: Be proud of what you write. Know that the only rule is to fill the page, usually in ten minutes, and you will have accomplished that!

HAVE FUN: Or maybe it's time to get a new hobby.

Now let's do some exercises …

Circle Game
one

Circle the one word that most appeals to you:
Alabama Banister Carousel Diesel Exorcist

Circle another word that appeals to you:
Flatulence Garage Harried Insensitive Jambalaya

Circle yet another word that you find appealing:
Keepsake Lamb Massage Nonsense Oriole

Use these three words in a story.
Start with: *Sometimes I feel just like a gerbil,*
running around and around on his wheel!

TAKE THE NEXT STEP

In terms of writing practice, what type of gerbil are you?

1. Running round and round on a wheel
2. Avoiding the wheel
3. Fearful of leaving the wheel
4. Running freely without need of a wheel

If writing practice were an airplane instead of a gerbil's wheel,
what would you do differently?

DAY **1**

RESOLUTION REVOLUTION ∽

Use each letter as you get to it. Start with: *New Year's resolutions make me ...*

N_____

_____E_____

_____W_____

Y_____

_____E_____

_____A_____

__R_____

_____S_____

_____R_____

_____E_____S_____

_____O_____

_____

_____L_____U_____

_____T_____

_____I_____

_____O_____

_____

_____N_____

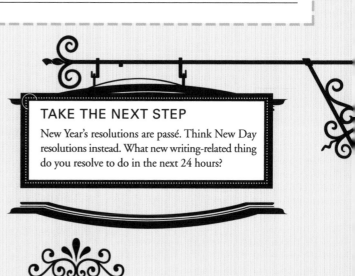

TAKE THE NEXT STEP

New Year's resolutions are passé. Think New Day resolutions instead. What new writing-related thing do you resolve to do in the next 24 hours?

DAY**2**

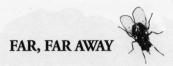

FAR, FAR AWAY

Think of a person who really bugs or annoys you. Think of a place you'd like to send this person. Then—mentally—send them there! With that in mind, start with:

The post card arrived … _____

_____

_____

_____

_____

_____

_____

_____

_____

_____

_____

_____

_____

_____

_____

_____

_____

𝒩

TAKE THE NEXT STEP

Describe the ideal place to write. Be very specific and detailed.

Go there in your mind the next time you write. See how your writing changes.

DAY3

Terrible Twos

You are two years old. Write from this perspective. Be childlike! PLAY!

Give yourself a name (with the initials C.A.T.):
Nickname:
Eye color:
Hair color:
Favorite food:
Siblings' names/ages:
How they treat you:
Thoughts on toilet training:

Start with: *Here I am stuck in my crib …*

TAKE THE NEXT STEP

In what area of your creativity are you stuck?

A new adhesive remover has been invented, guaranteed to get you unstuck. What's the first creative step you'll take now that you're free?

DAY**4**

Ship Shape

Write until you fill in the entire shape.
There are no lines, allowing you to be
creative and free. Start with:

The ship's sail …

TAKE THE NEXT STEP

When in need of perking up, some folks go boating,
some play air hockey, others listen to loud music. List
four things you do.

Next time you are lethargic, do one of these to perk up before returning to your writing with renewed energy.

THOSE WERE THE DAYS

Finish the story. Start with:

Back in 1938, before ...

TAKE THE NEXT STEP

If there are 1,938 reasons NOT to write ...
Name one reason TO write that outweighs
them all:

*So, what are you waiting for? See how much
you can write before the year 2038!*

DAY**6**

YOU MAY HAVE ALREADY WON

You have received a believable-looking, business-sized white envelope in the mail. The return address is from a company called Peerless. Printed on the envelope, in bright red letters, are the words "You May Have Already Won." Tell the story of what it is you may have won—or what it is you didn't win. Tell what you do with this envelope.

Start with: *Life takes some funny twists and turns …*

TAKE THE NEXT STEP

You've just arrived at a two week writing retreat that you won. Write a note home listing all you plan to accomplish.

Now, do one (or all) of these things, right from wherever you are!

MY CONDIMENTS TO THE CHEF!

Soy Sauce

Mayonnaise Mustard Relish

Pickle Hot Peppers

Ketchup

**Use all of these words
in a piece that starts:**

HIS TASTE IN WOMEN WAS ...

TAKE THE NEXT STEP

To make Russian dressing, you mix ketchup, mayo, and relish. List three pieces of unfinished writing you can combine to come up with one new completed work. *Try it!*

FICTIONARY

Write a dictionary-style definition for the word
EC•DYS•I•AST (pronounced eckDIZeeAST).

Use **ECDYSIAST** with your fictitious definition
in a story. Start with:

It all started when …

TAKE THE NEXT STEP

Write a definition of the word *writer*
so that when someone picks up the
dictionary, your name comes to
mind immediately.

*Write your definition on ten slips of
paper and insert them (under* writer*),
in the dictionaries of nine friends or
relatives. Put the last one in your own
dictionary.*

(The real definition of ecdysiast (n) is a striptease artist! How close was your definition?)

DAY**9**

Following Directions

Use the directional words as you get to them. Start with: Just like the little red caboose...

Up

Right

Left

Down

TAKE THE NEXT STEP

The Little Red Caboose said, "I think I can, I think I can." Write down a facet of your writing craft that would be helped by repeating "I know I can, I know I can."

Say it over and over until you believe you can. Then do it.

Very Touching

Think of a slinky. Write four textures that come to mind.

1. _____
2. _____
3. _____
4. _____

Now think of a scarf. Write four textures that come to mind.

1. _____
2. _____
3. _____
4. _____

Use all these in a story that begins:

Late night city streets were the perfect backdrop for . . .

_____
_____
_____
_____
_____
_____
_____
_____
_____
_____
_____
_____
_____
_____
_____
_____
_____
_____
_____
_____
_____
_____

TAKE THE NEXT STEP

What's the ideal motivational backdrop to hang behind you when you write?

Find (or take) a picture, draw, or make a collage that ignites this mood. Hang it behind you. When you need a bit of motivation, take a mini-vacation and turn around and look at it.

Spoiled Rotten

List six disgusting things you've found in your refrigerator (or have heard others describe they have found in theirs):

Use all six in a story. Start with:
Whenever he mentions Paris …

TAKE THE NEXT STEP

Many wonderful ideas come while doing mundane tasks. Hang paper and a pencil on your refrigerator to record ideas that come to you while washing dishes; in your bathroom for ideas that come in the shower; and in the car for long-distance drive inspirations. (Pull over to write, please!)

Do it now. Don't miss out on a single creative writing idea!

You (SLisa) speak this language to torture your two younger sisters, SPatty and SLorna. Write in this language.

Start with:

*When I babysit for you spipsqueaks
on Saturday night I am going to …*

You have made up your own language where you put the letter S in front of all words beginning with your initials, L and P.

You are a 13-year-old girl named Lisa Palluzzi.

TAKE THE NEXT STEP

Who are you when it comes to writing practice?

1. Underpaid teenage babysitter
2. Nanny from Europe
3. Retiree earning supplemental income
4. Well-behaved child
5. Poorly-behaved child
6. Parents who are away

In order to be more productive, gain rewards, and still take care of yourself, who else might you be?

DAY **13**

TESTING
1-2-3

1. Choose ONE word that most appeals to you:

Trophy   Bible   Inhale   Giraffe

Weed   Lava   Crush   Banana   Mask   Gas

Fender

2. Choose ONE setting that most appeals to you:

At a circus

During a war   In a space station

Under a full moon   On a beach   At a park

3. Choose ONE starting phrase that most appeals to you:

If I could stop   I once asked

The first day   If you must know

The hurricane neared

Start your story with this phrase,
and incorporate the setting and word.

TAKE THE NEXT STEP

Many things come in threes, including three-word expressions like "live, love, laugh" and "hip, hip, hooray." List as many as you can think of.

Include all these phrases in a story. Set a timer for ten minutes. Ready, set, go!

DAY **14**

Idioms Delight
{One}

Start with the idiom: *I don't usually hit the ground running...*

_____

_____

_____

_____

In your conclusion, use this idiomatic expression: *That's the way the cookie crumbles.*

TAKE THE NEXT STEP

If you approached your writing as if you were a pastry chef, what would you do differently?

Try it next time you write. See if your writing is different.

DAY **15**

Knot Now

Finish the story. Start with: *She adjusted his bow tie ...*

_____

_____

_____

_____

_____

_____

_____

_____

_____

_____

_____

_____

TAKE THE NEXT STEP

In terms of writing, finish these:

I am not _____.

I am not _____.

I am not _____.

I am not _____.

Cross out the negative ones. Sometimes we need to be reminded to speak positively about ourselves. Next time you're asked if you're a writer, don't hem and haw or make excuses. Simply say, "I am."

DAY 16

Building Blocks

Use these six items like blocks and build a story.
Start with: *The last time I ...*

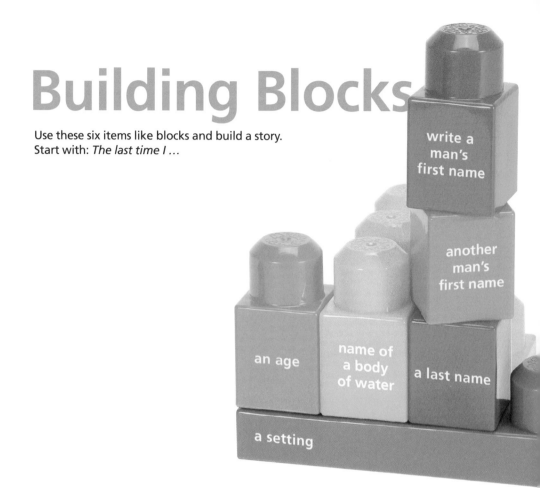

- write a man's first name
- another man's first name
- an age
- name of a body of water
- a last name
- a setting

TAKE THE NEXT STEP

List four ways you can build time into your life to do more writing. Perhaps you'll get up ten minutes earlier or write in line at the supermarket.

Get out your calendar and schedule them in now!

DAY **17**

ONE SILL A BULL

This is a fave of mine 'cause it makes you dig for words. Each word in this piece must be ONE SILL A BULL. Start with: *The bull ...*

TAKE THE NEXT STEP

In terms of creative writing, which step in the process brings out the stubborn bull in you? Getting started? Writing the middle? Finishing? Editing? Sending it into the world? *Record ideas to gently treat this phase more like a calm lamb. Try one and see if it helps.*

DAY **18**

Back In Time

Write about an important, big-time event in your childhood. Write in first person as if you are, once again, that age and it just happened. Use child-appropriate language. Don't worry if it turns out to be more fiction than fact. Start with: Yesterday was ...

Now write about the same event, but as an adult looking back. Don't worry if the story changes this time as you go with the flow. Start with: If I could go back in time to the day when ...

TAKE THE NEXT STEP

Go back in time and list six memories from various Januarys in your life.

Use these to prompt future writings.

Craven Lion

See how many words—of four letters or more—you can make from the letters in the word CRAVEN, which means cowardly. Aim for fifteen words. (A full list appears at the bottom of the page.) List them here.

Try to use all fifteen words in a story which begins: *I was craving* …

TAKE THE NEXT STEP

Both cowardly feelings and obsessive cravings appear in our nighttime dreams. Keeping a dream journal is good fodder for writers. Record a recent dream to use as a spark for future writing.

(carve, crave, rave, raven, cave, cavern, vane, cane, aver, crane, care, race, acre, earn, near)

You are in a bus depot in New York.

A gypsy appears out of nowhere and hands you this card:

Use all seven elements that appear on the card in a story that begins:

It almost seems impossible for me to go back to that split second when ...

TAKE THE NEXT STEP

Make your writing more clear and interesting in a split second by changing from passive voice to active voice. Compare these examples.

Dull and passive: My car **was driven** to Florida by Jake.

More alive and active: Jake **drove** my car to Florida.

Go back through this exercise (and others you've done in the book) and change passive voice to active voice.

Reminiscing - One

Imagine talking to a friend from your childhood. Retell stories and reminisce about favorite times. Use the starting phrases provided.

Do you remember the time we tried …

Do you remember the time we called …

Do you remember the time we asked …

Do you remember the time we joined …

TAKE THE NEXT STEP

Positive self-talk is a great way to achieve goals. Create a writing goal. (No negative words, please.)

Every morning and evening after brushing your teeth, repeat it aloud to yourself. You CAN make it happen.

DAY**22**

Zounds of Sounds

Use the sounds as you come to them. Start with:

The guru told us to …

TICK TOCK

CHIME

CRASH

PIN-DROP

TINKLING

THUD

BOING

SHHHH!

SCRATCHING

TAKE THE NEXT STEP

If you were a creative writing guru, what daily practice would you make mandatory so your devotees will become the best possible writers?

Do you currently practice what you preach? Why or why not?

Remember Me?

This is a personal ad from a local newspaper.

Write how the scenario unfolds. Start with:
I don't usually …

(Thanks to Teresa Piccari for the exercise idea on this page.)

CHRIS – LAST TUES, 8:45 pm – BOOK BIN CAFÉ Want to thank you again for the cappuccino. You made my day. Haven't been able to get you off my mind, especially your hair. Went back three times to look for you. Kicking myself for not asking for your phone number. Pat. Box 8281.

TAKE THE NEXT STEP

List those who have helped or influenced you on your path to becoming a successful writer.

Send each a note of thanks. It'll make them feel good and keep you serious about your craft.
(Thanks to Teresa Piccari for this exercise idea.)

Famous Firsts - One

*Finish the story. Start with: We had spent the afternoon in a café
on the Rue Saint-Jacques, a spring afternoon just like any other.*

(This first line is from *A Certain Smile* by Francoise Sagan.)

TAKE THE NEXT STEP

When you become rich and famous, what's the first charity to
which you'll make a donation?

*Get out a check right now, fill in the amount you plan to give, sign
it, then write VOID over the signature. Keep it by your desk as a re-
minder of one of the ways that your success can and will help others.*

DAY25

Adventurous Adverbs

Use the adverbs as you get to them.

Start with: We left from ...

madly

happily

insanely

mystically

desperately

TAKE THE NEXT STEP

Continue the adventure: Select one sentence from this story and use it as a starter for another writing. To up the ante, this time use all ten of these adverbs in the new story: Unfortunately, Adamantly, Stealthily, Methodically, Furiously, Erratically, Mysteriously, Stingingly, Virtually, Belatedly.

Dear Diary - One

CIRCLE ONE AGE OPTION:

12 yr. old girl

64 yr. old beekeeper

20 yr. old college student

42 yr. old movie star

6 yr. old boy

CIRCLE ONE LOCATION OPTION:

Live on a farm

Live in a penthouse

Live in a mansion

Live on the streets

Live with aunt and uncle

You are now this person and this is where you live.

You just found a diary from 1864. Let the story unfold. Start with:

Some people might not have opened ...

TAKE THE NEXT STEP

If you knew no one would ever read what you write, would you:

Not write at all
Write a bit less
Write a lot more

How else would this affect your writing?

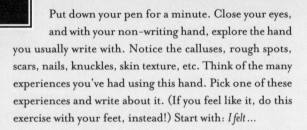

HANDS DOWN

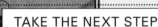

Put down your pen for a minute. Close your eyes, and with your non-writing hand, explore the hand you usually write with. Notice the calluses, rough spots, scars, nails, knuckles, skin texture, etc. Think of the many experiences you've had using this hand. Pick one of these experiences and write about it. (If you feel like it, do this exercise with your feet, instead!) Start with: *I felt…*

TAKE THE NEXT STEP

Your body holds many stories. Jot down two stories that your knees might tell. How about your chin?

Next time you're looking for something to write, choose one of these.

PICK AN AGE BETWEEN 2-88:

EYE COLOR:

HAIR COLOR:

NAME OF A CITY/TOWN:

TYPE OF RESIDENCE/HOUSE:

FIRST NAME STARTING WITH G:

LAST NAME STARTING WITH S:

PROMINENT PHYSICAL FEATURE:

QUIRK/MANNERISM:

You are now officially this character. Start with:

I remember when the power went off ...

WHAT A CHARACTER!

TAKE THE NEXT STEP

Don't worry if you feel like you're having a creativity power outage. This is a vital part of the creative cycle, called the receptive phase. When you're in this phase, it's important to relax and let ideas/inspirations flow through you. One will spark the next part of the cycle, called the active phase. Learn to enjoy both parts of the cycle. Go out and receive!

DAY**29**

A PIECE OF FURNITURE

_____

A FOOD PRODUCT

_____

A WORD ABOUT RELIGION

_____

A TYPE OF SHOE

_____

USE THESE SIX WORDS IN YOUR STORY. START WITH:

I REMEMBER CATCHING …

A BODY PART

A SPORTS VERB

_____

DAY**30**

Fair FARE

Finish the story. Start with: *In his rearview mirror, the cab driver saw …*

TAKE THE NEXT STEP

Rather than beat ourselves up over where we are not, or what we still have to learn, it's healthy to remind ourselves how much we know and how far we've come. Look back and write two things you know now that you wish you had known when you started writing.

OVALTEEN

Let the shapes aid your imagination as you write. There is a starting phrase provided for the first "football."

Other directions follow.

Just like a football, I ...

Use the last sentence from the piece you just completed to start a new writing in the second football.

TAKE THE NEXT STEP

Describe your current writing practice as if it were a colored shape. (Ex: a soft 26-sided brown blob with scattered neon pink polka dots inside.) What would you prefer it to look like? Get some markers or crayons and draw it.

Sink Your Teeth Into It

Finish the story. Start with: *My teeth were chattering…*

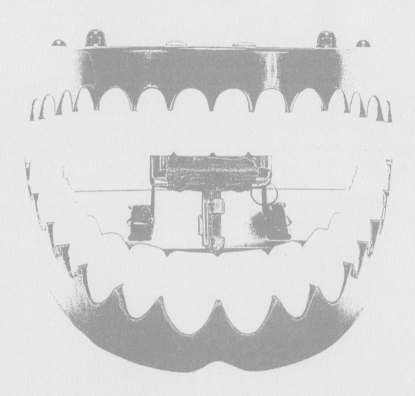

TAKE THE NEXT STEP

Describe your current writing attitude as a type of food. Is it something you'd like to sink your teeth into? What can you do to turn your writing attitude into a food you'd like to sink your teeth into? What's your new writing attitude food?

DAY**33**

Stream of Consciousness

Start with the word CONSCIOUS and free associate. Write down whatever comes to mind. Example: pillow, sleep, dream, flying, pink sky, aliens, music, Beethoven, rock ...

Circle eight interesting words and use them in a story. Start with:
The sparkling trout stream ...

CONSCIOUS

TAKE THE NEXT STEP

Free associate again, starting with the word COMMITMENT.

Do these words reveal anything new to you about your writing self?

CAN YOU BELIEVE IT?

Finish these four short shorts. Starters are provided.

I can't believe I was afraid of …

I can't believe I was intimidated by …

I can't believe she never told me …

I can't believe how many years it's been since …

TAKE THE NEXT STEP

Like beliefs, Haiku reflects your unique life view. Compose a Haiku about belief, using this basic syllabic formula:

5 syllables
7 syllables
5 syllables

No Bull

You are a matador from Spain, visiting Los Angeles. You are smitten by an off-duty waitress whom you met at a bar. Let the story unfold. Start with: *Where I come from, women ...*

TAKE THE NEXT STEP

Coming from the point of view of your favorite author (dead or alive), write about the above story as if he or she were positively reviewing it.

Scribble ONE

This exercise uses letter tiles like a familiar word game. When you get to a letter and use it as the FIRST LETTER of a word, you get two points. Try for 50 points!

His eyes …

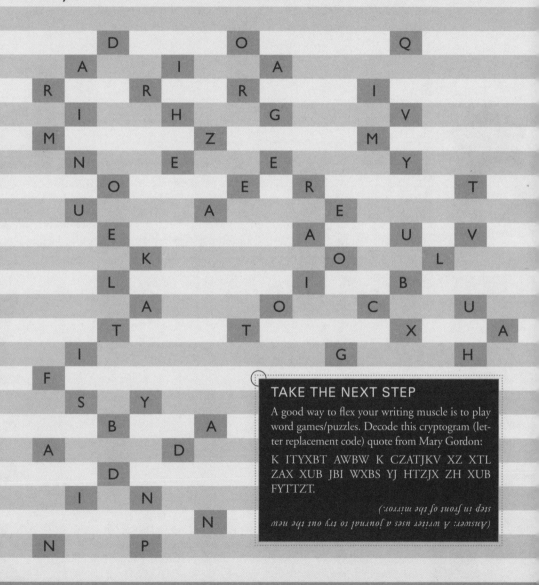

DRIBBLING
BANANAS

List eight action verbs from sports here (ending in -ing):

1. _____
2. _____
3. _____
4. _____
5. _____
6. _____
7. _____
8. _____

List eight common everyday plural nouns here:

1. _____
2. _____
3. _____
4. _____
5. _____
6. _____
7. _____
8. _____

Now draw arrows connecting these verbs and nouns in unusual combinations. You'll end up with things like dribbling bananas, squatting shoes, shooting lima beans, etc. Pick one (or more) of these combinations and use the images in a story that begins: The alarm went off ...

TAKE THE NEXT STEP

Have you written "morning pages" as per Julia Cameron's book *The Artist's Way*? It's a great way to clear your mind so nothing stands between you and your creativity the rest of the day. Put a pen and three sheets of paper by the alarm clock. As soon as the alarm goes off, write until all three pages are filled. Observe how you feel different the rest of the day.

Shake-Spear

Use all these words that were coined by the bard:

Arch-villain   Madcap   Gallantry   Trippingly   Pageantry

Start with: He laid his right hand on the spear …

CatchUp One

Finish the story. Start with: *The first time I saw him, he was digging ketchup out of a bottle with a knife …*

TAKE THE NEXT STEP

Dig deeper into the main character in this story. What does she or he really care about? What motivates him or her? How is he or she like you?

DAY**40**

Catch-Up (2)

Finish the story. Start with: *The first time I saw her she was teaching third graders that ketchup is a vegetable …*

TAKE THE NEXT STEP

Do you believe writing is:

Teachable?
Something you're born with?
Learned only by doing?
Genetic?
What is your opinion about teaching or learning writing? How does this affect the way you approach writing?

DAY**41**

Gotta Lotta

When Louis Armstrong was asked what jazz is, he replied, "Man, if you gotta ask, you'll never know." Use this quote in a story. There's no need to reference jazz or Louis Armstrong, unless you want to. Start with:

The captain shouted, "Anchors aweigh, my boys," and we …

TAKE THE NEXT STEP

What things do you feel you 'gotta' have in place in your life before you can seriously write?

Do you realize it's possible for you to seriously write without any of these, other than a pen and paper?

Staring Contest

For this exercise, **STARE** straight ahead. **DON'T LOOK** down at the page. Focus your eyes on an object and keep them there. Don't worry about your handwriting or neatness. Just enjoy the **TRANCE**-like experience. Start with:

I see ...

TAKE THE NEXT STEP

List what frightens or intimidates you about facing a blank page.

Do you realize you made all that up?

Now write what excites you about a blank page.

Feels better, doesn't it?

Love Letter Story

Make up a sentence, or the beginning of a sentence, containing words beginning with the following letters: T S L M A B. Examples: Tracy Stone loved marbles and baubles. Or The sprite leprechaun missed a beat ... Use this as a beginning for a story.

T_____ S_____
L_____ M _____ A_____
B_____
_____
_____
_____
_____
_____
_____
_____
_____

TAKE THE NEXT STEP

What do you love about reading?

Everything you read was created by a writer. You, too, have the talent and commitment to bring this joy to others. Keep writing and you will give more folks more reasons to love reading.

(*Love Story* by Erich Segal begins with words with these six letters, *"That she loved Mozart and Bach ..."*)

DAY **44**

My Money Valentine

Write a Valentine's Day letter to the wealthiest person you've ever heard of. Butter them up big time, flatter them to your heart's content, and then ask for something outrageous!

Start with:

Dear _____,

You are, without a doubt, the most ...

TAKE THE NEXT STEP

We all have expectations and excuses about money. List some of yours. How do these influence your writing? Picture placing one excuse inside a balloon. Let go of it today!

Memory Lane

Take a few short trips down memory lane. Write the truth, embellished memories, or make everything up! Use the starting phrases to get you started down the path.

I remember learning ...

I remember biting ...

I remember the balloons ...

I remember falling ...

TAKE THE NEXT STEP

"I remember" often takes us back to childhood where we learned by using all our senses, especially touch and taste. Finish this: *I remember the taste of ...*

Tomorrow, before you do anything else, finish this: *I remember the smell of ...*

BUBBLE RAP I

Create a dialogue between two people, using the speech bubbles provided. There are two colors, one per person. There is a starter to get you on your way.

If you could ...

TAKE THE NEXT STEP

Do you approach writing as a not-yet popped; totally popped; or now-being popped piece of bubble wrap? Describe your writing practice in terms of being bubble wrap. What's your size? Where've you been? Where're you going? What'll happen next? How are you being handled?

NUTS & BOLTS

Got a screw loose • Sharp as a tack • Nail it down • On the level • Flew off the handle

Use these five expressions in this piece.
Start with: It hit me like a ton of bricks …

TAKE THE NEXT STEP

Get down to the nuts and bolts of writing—nailing down quotation marks:

1. Represent text as speech
2. Indicate material excerpted from another writer
3. Indicate titles of poems, essays, short stories
4. Periods and commas go inside
5. Colons, semicolons, dashes, question marks, and exclamation points go outside unless they're part of the quotation.

Make your repairs.

Choices, Choices

CHOOSE ONE:
A. I'd like to be able to fly using my own powers
B. I'd like to be able to make myself invisible

You now possess this super power for the story you are about to write. Start with: It was just a teeny-weeny little lie ...

TAKE THE NEXT STEP

Try this teeny-weeny exercise: Set a timer for ten minutes, get comfortable—but not too comfy—and think about writing. Do not write, take notes, or jot anything down—no matter how much you want to during the ten minutes. Just think about writing ...

What happened for you? Surprised?

Weird Words—One

Use the words **ATMU** and **BUKRA** in your story—even though you probably don't know what they mean. Set your story in Alaska in December. Start with: *Lapis sky, green palms, sand the color of pale gold …*

TAKE THE NEXT STEP

If you think Alaska in December is cold, imagine how you're treating yourself when you belittle what you've written. Read aloud (in a nice, warm, gentle tone) what you just wrote. Tell yourself (aloud) all the things you like about it: striking imagery, good word choice, nice handwriting, clever ending, etc. Do this with everything you write!

P.S. **ATMU** is Egyptian for twilight and **BUKRA** is Egyptian for tomorrow.

Once Upon a Time

Ah! The classic opener! Finish the story.
Start with: Once upon a time …

TAKE THE NEXT STEP

List six memories from the Februarys of your life.

Use these to prompt further writings.

SWAMP THING

Finish the story.
Start with: *Down by the swamp …* _____

_____

_____

_____

_____

_____

_____

_____

_____

_____

_____

_____

_____

_____

_____

_____

_____

_____

_____

_____

_____

_____

TAKE THE NEXT STEP

Set a writing deadline now and ask a core support group to check in regularly with you. We're all swamped, but most everyone can find time to leave a voice message or send an e-mail. Tell them exactly what to say so it's a mindless task. Example: "Hi. Checking in to make sure you're on track and to let you know I'm here if you have any challenges."

"quote, unquote"

"THIS IS NOT A NOVEL TO BE TOSSED ASIDE LIGHTLY. IT SHOULD BE THROWN WITH GREAT FORCE."

—DOROTHY PARKER

Use this quote somewhere in your piece.
Start with: I HATE THE TEXTURE OF...

TAKE THE NEXT STEP

Search through books or on the Internet for a quote that motivates you to write. Copy it here and also on a piece of paper.

Carry it with you until you've committed it to memory. Then pass the paper to someone else would benefit from this wisdom. Ask them to memorize it and pass it on again.

SNAPSHOTS *one*

Photos are a great way to capture memories. But we don't always have a camera with us. Write quick "word snapshots" as substitutes for the following topics. Try to capture colors, textures, and expressions. Use your own life story … or make them up!

A childhood birthday party

A wedding

Winning an award

A garden

TAKE THE NEXT STEP

If someone took a snapshot of you while you were writing today, what would the caption read? Now write a caption for a snapshot taken while you are in flow. Make this caption come true when you write tomorrow.

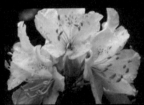

Metamorphosis

Finish the story. Start with:

Like a butterfly, she magically …

TAKE THE NEXT STEP

If you treated all your creative desires and demands as if you were a butterfly, what would you do differently?

Next time you write, spread your wings and see how your writing changes.

DAY**55**

YES OR NO

Write a question that can be answered YES or NO. Rather than fret over it, we're going to ask a pendulum for the answer. Begin writing about your question now.

Start with: The pendulum says NO …

Oops, I'm sorry, the pendulum says YES …
Go back and write more!

TAKE THE NEXT STEP

You never know until you ask … Do something today toward putting your work out into the world: Submit an article to a local newspaper, a poem to a literary journal, a query to an agent, a proposal to a publisher, an entry to a writing contest, an essay to an online 'zine. Just do it! It's time for the world to read your words.

DAY**56**

Shape Up

Use these shorts to get in shape. Use the shapes provided as part of your creation. Write between the shapes as well! There are four starters provided. If you can, make all your short pieces have a common theme.

Love is a trap, and I am ...

The way I see it ...

It's not what he said, it's what he ...

If I could ...

TAKE THE NEXT STEP

Combine getting in shape with writing by doing a cardiovascular exercise before you write. While your heart's still pounding hard and you're still sweating, immediately put pen to paper. Before you try it, how do you think this will affect your writing?

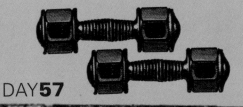

DAY**57**

BROWN TOWN

Look around you. Notice all the BROWN things.

Write down the first six you see:

1. _____   4. _____

2. _____   5. _____

3.   6.

Use all six. Start with: **I AM USUALLY OBLIVIOUS TO …**

my eyes are brown... my teeth are not

TAKE THE NEXT STEP

Very often we're oblivious to the multitude of sounds (or silences) around us. Take a moment now and simply listen. Then record all you hear.

Incorporate sound/hearing into your next writing.

DAY**58**

Freshman-itis

You're a high school freshman. Write from this low-man-on-the-totem-pole perspective. Be a teenager!

Use these initials for a name: **N.A.K.**

A nickname:

Eye color:

Hair color:

Nicknames of best friends:

How they treat you:

How you treat them:

Favorite food:

Thoughts on sports:

Start with: *It hasn't been the best day, but it certainly hasn't been the worst …*

TAKE THE NEXT STEP

Not every day can be the 'best' day. Write one affirmative thing about your creative self from the last 24 hours.

If you like this, keep an affirmation journal where you record something positive about yourself for the day—every day.

Sincerely Yours

Start with: *Dear Dolores, I know it has been 37 years since I have been in touch*

TAKE THE NEXT STEP

If you currently have a goal to meet (if not, set one right now), go to an online greeting card site. Send a timed e-greeting of congratulations to yourself, scheduled to arrive the last day of the goal. Knowing you sent the card will keep you on track. If you aren't online, give a pre-stamped card to a friend to mail to you two days before your goal date.

MARCH MUMBLE

Use the speech sounds as you get to them. Start with: We marched ...

oooh

harumph   pssst

heh

shhhhh

ahhhhh

hmmm

whew

TAKE THE NEXT STEP

Turn on the radio to a music station you don't usually listen to. Listen until a song ends. How is what you just wrote similar to the song you heard?

How are they different?

Exposing yourself to new things helps your writing grow.

DAY**61**

Happy *Endings*

Use the last sentences at the bottom of the page to conclude your story.

... *He* left, and Mike pushed back his halo and got to work. He could see a lot of changes he wanted to make —

(Last 2 sentences from *Stranger In A Strange Land* by Robert A. Heinlein.)

TAKE THE NEXT STEP

What excites you about ending a project?

What scares you about ending a project?

List ideas on how you can turn this fear into excitement every time.

DAY**62**

Flavor

of the month

Write down twelve flavors:

_____ _____ _____ _____

_____ _____ _____ _____

_____ _____ _____ _____

Use all twelve flavors in this piece. Start with:
The sparkling water was ...

TAKE THE NEXT STEP

Sending marshmallow-fudge-swirl-double-cone prose to an editor whose preference is a small dish of lime sorbet poetry usually results in a rejection. List publications/publishers with whom your writing flavors and portions are compatible.

Send your writing to one.

VERRRRRRRRRY SLEEEEEEEPY

Write, and whenever you get to a word, use it!!
Start with: *The hypnotist promised he could help …*

_____

_____circles_____

_____

_____stairs_____

_____huge_____

_____

_____tiny_____

_____sparkle_____

_____ice_____

_____

_____fire_____

_____alarm_____

_____

_____spiral_____

TAKE THE NEXT STEP

You've been hypnotized to stop everything and write every morning.
Make it the first thing you do every day for two minutes a day.

DAY**64**

CONSTRUCTION WORKER COMMENTARIES

You are a
construction worker.
Complete each of these
four shorts in his voice.

Guns are . . .

The right to . . .

Stephen King is . . .

Republicans are . . .

TAKE THE NEXT STEP

Construction workers don't have the luxury of going back through
their projects to redo what doesn't work. Fortunately, writers do. Even
so, many writers fear the editing process. If you view it as such, it's a
most positive opportunity. Now go back through these four writings
and enjoy yourself as you edit by deleting all unnecessary words.

DAY**65**

Take a Seat

Finish the story. Start with: His chair...

TAKE THE NEXT STEP

Sit up and use the good posture you were taught in school, hold your pen properly, originate slow breaths from your diaphragm (below your rib cage), and copy a sentence from this page here.

Feel the difference? It's all part of the craft.

No Clowning Around

Finish the story.
Start with:
Clowns make me …

TAKE THE NEXT STEP

Had the audience been different, the above exercise might have appeared as follows:

Commence here and bring this narrative to completion: *The effect of a jester on one is …*

Get out a thesaurus or dictionary and change some words (in this exercise or in another writing you've done) to better resonate with your intended audience.

Dreamy

USE THE SHAPES AS YOU LIKE.
A STARTER IS PROVIDED.

I remember
dreaming ...

TAKE THE NEXT STEP

Don't cloud your writing by mumbling when you read it
aloud. Stand tall and read this page out loud, enunciating
every word. Read it over and over until you are certain that
listeners will hear the pride you take in your creativity. Now
do the same with a polished piece of writing. If you don't
have one, find one to edit and then read it aloud with pride.

All my Life is a Circle
– One

Circle the one word that most appeals to you:

Helium

Circus

Rings

Balloon

Popcorn

Circle another word that appeals to you:

Clown

Elephant

Laugh

Top

Tent

Circle yet another word that you find appealing:

Tame

Tightrope

Acrobat

Master

Lion

Use these three words in a story. Start with: **She shrugged her shoulders and said, "I don't know why …**

TAKE THE NEXT STEP

Get a marker, crayon, or colored pencil and draw circular flowing swirls all over this page until you can no longer read what you just wrote. How did it feel when you were doing it? Was it easy for you, or hard?

Letting go is different for every person and for every piece. Remember, what you write in this book is practice.

KLEPTOMANIA

Find a book or magazine and steal the first line to begin your piece on this page. If you don't have a book or magazine handy, use this starter:

HE HOPPED OFF THE HORSE LIKE A HOLLYWOOD COWBOY ...

TAKE THE NEXT STEP

Stealing from the lives of others is what writers do. List three things you've read or heard about others that would work well in a story.

Combine them all into a story you write in the next ten minutes. Set a timer now!

Congrats

Write a letter congratulating yourself on something you did especially well today. Perhaps it is staying on a diet OR avoiding someone who usually gives you grief OR taking procrastination to a new high OR doing this exercise!!

Dear _____,

I commend you on the fine job you did today ...

TAKE THE NEXT STEP

Write an ideal job description that uses all your talents, pays extraordinarily well, and allows you to wake up happy every day.

Sometimes just putting it out into the universe will make it happen. (Be careful what you ask for!) Read it out loud.

Word Wok

List five foreign words here (make sure you know the meaning of the words):

1.
2.
3.
4.
5.

Use all five words in a story that takes place on a new planet.
Begin with the phrase: *It was Halloween* …

TAKE THE NEXT STEP

Think of four words or expressions that are used by your family or the people where you grew up. (Ex: Outten the lights)

1.
2.
3.
4.

This is a great way to add local color to your writing. Use all four in a mini-autobiography.

GOMER

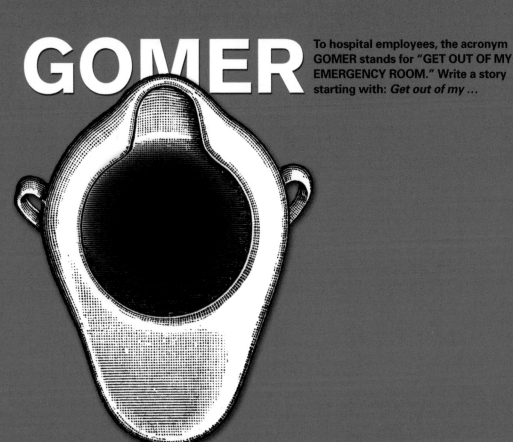

To hospital employees, the acronym GOMER stands for "GET OUT OF MY EMERGENCY ROOM." Write a story starting with: *Get out of my ...*

The Great Divide

Use both starters.

Even when we're not lost, she …

He never stops to ask for directions …

TAKE THE NEXT STEP

If you were to divide your life in the last year into two parts, writing and not-writing, what percent was spent writing?

What percent was spent not writing?

Starting today for the next year, what percentage would you like to spend writing?

Block out the time now—for the entire year!

society, for exam...
to a   project, it adds realis...
...itec-   One recent project...
...t has   the classroom and the real w...

You are the journal or diary of an 18-year old girl. She's been writing in you daily about dieting, school, her ex-best-friend, an upcoming dance and one particular boy. You're tired of her complaints and her whining. So while she is asleep one night, you write back.

Dear _____,
It has been ...

TAKE THE NEXT STEP

Write a one-sentence journal entry in observation of your writing process:

If you like this, keep a separate process journal in which you record daily thoughts about your writing process. (Thanks to Rachel Simon for this idea.)

DAY 75

REVENGE OF THE JOURNAL

RAPID RECALL

Write the first thing that comes to mind, even if
it's not at all true. Don't stop to think. Write fast!
Use the starters provided.

I recall a time when …

The product recall …

I recall writing …

TAKE THE NEXT STEP

Recall six memories that happened during the Marches
of your life.

Use these to prompt further writings.

Lion-Hearted By Day

Finish the story. Start with: *Her name was Kimba and I ...*

TAKE THE NEXT STEP

Are you most creative in the morning, afternoon, evening, night? What about this time of day helps you be creative? What can you do to mimic this set-up to enjoy similar writing conditions during other times of the day? *Try it.*

Who, What, When, Where ... And Why not??

Use the five items in a story. Start with: *It's hard to believe, but ...*

Who: A king
What: A chain
When: Daybreak
Where: Airport
Expression: "Why not?"

TAKE THE NEXT STEP

For whom do you write? Describe your mental picture of your audience.

Find/take a picture showing your audience giving you a standing ovation. Place it in this book to help you stay clear and motivated about your commitment to writing.

Double Dare

Finish the story.
Start with: *She said, "I double dare you …"*

TAKE THE NEXT STEP

Name one thing you've done that others might interpret as daring or risky, but you see merely as a path to a solution or a determined part of your process.

How often do you do things like this?

Would you be happier if you did them more or less often? Make that happen.

STATES OF MIND

Use the shape if you choose. Finish the story. Start with:
I was in a California state of mind yet stuck on a farm in Iowa …

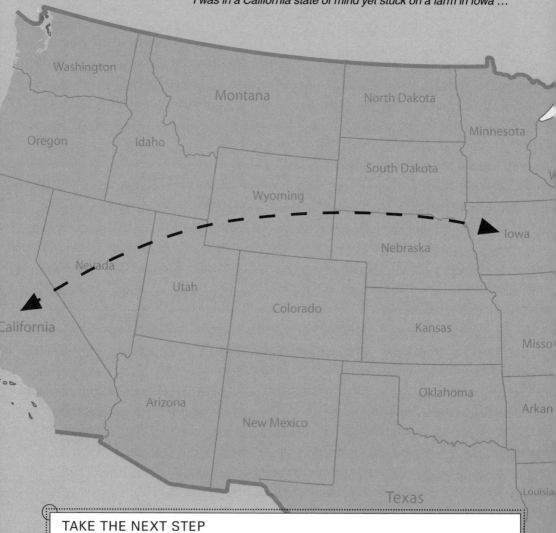

TAKE THE NEXT STEP

State a fear that keeps you from writing your personal truth.

Let go of the fear a little bit every time you write. Don't jump off the high wire without a net. Take it nice and easy by simply letting go of a little more every time you write.

Favorite Color

Pick a color you like. Write it (or shades of it) inside each bracketed space on the page.
Now fill in the rest.

Start with: [   ] like a

[   ]

[   ]

[   ]

[   ]

[   ]

[   ]

[   ]

TAKE THE NEXT STEP

When you are writing in flow, what color crayon or marker are you? Why? To jumpstart or keep your
flow going, get a marker or crayon this color. Write with it tomorrow—ALL DAY!

Narrow Escape

Sometimes the width between the lines influences what you are writing.
Try this one with very narrow spaces. Start with: *Escaping was the only …*

TAKE THE NEXT STEP

Write about a place where you can escape (in your mind's eye) when things get rough. Use all five senses so someone else can actually see, feel, hear, taste, smell it.

TAG-1

In Pennsylvania most license plates are three letters and four numbers. Example: AAJ 9037. For this exercise use the three letters as the first letters of the three beginning words in your story. Example: Alice Always Joked. Use the four digit number, 9037, somewhere in your story.

Start here: A_____ A_____ J_____ ...

TAKE THE NEXT STEP

You are about to start a game of writing-practice tag. You are "it" first, so you must immediately fill two pages with writing. Once you're done, tag a writer friend to be "it." Hand them two blank sheets of paper and explain the simple rule of writing two pages before tagging someone else to be "it." And so on ...

REBUS
TERMINAL

**Instead of words, this exercise has symbols.
Use them as you come to them. Start with:
THE BUS PULLED INTO THE TERMINAL IN …**

No If's, And's or Don'ts

DON'T use any of these words in your story:

COLD CHILL SNOW ICE SLEET FLURRY WINTER FREEZING SHIVER

Start with: **We** arrived in the Arctic at noon and immediately ventured out into the 30 feet of blinding white ...

TAKE THE NEXT STEP

Fill in the blanks.

If I had _____, then I'd write _____.

If _____ didn't matter, I'd write _____.

If I was guaranteed _____, I'd write _____.

Assume one of these is true for the next 24 hours. Now write your heart out.

Philately
Will Get You Nowhere

You are a devout stamp collector.
You meet the person of your dreams and make a date.
Unlike your date, you are nice as can be.
Tell the story. Start with:

I wish I could turn back the hands of time ...

Use the line,

"Philately will get you nowhere"

in your conclusion.

TAKE THE NEXT STEP

If you approached your writing the way a devoted philatelist tends to his/her stamp collection, what would you do differently? *Try this approach the next time you write and see what's different!*

snooping

Think back to a time when you looked someplace that you shouldn't have. Example: looking in the drawer of the nightstand of the people you were babysitting for. Write about this episode, and don't forget to embellish it and tell what you found!

Start with:
When I opened ...

TAKE THE NEXT STEP

Opening lines must grab the reader on many levels. Go back through this book and choose an opening line you wrote. Rewrite it and continue to polish it until it shines.

LOST AND FOUND

Write with crayons or very thick markers and finish this story. Start with:
The moment I found that teeny, tiny little …

Write six sounds that are touching, like a baby's coo or lovers' lips meeting in a quiet kiss.

_____   _____

_____   _____

_____   _____

Use them all in a story that begins:

LATELY I HAVE BEEN UNABLE TO TOLERATE …

TAKE THE NEXT STEP

Read aloud what you just wrote, listening to the sounds as if they were music. Circle words, phrases, sentences that sound "off." Go back and change them. Continue to reread the piece aloud, making changes until it flows and sounds consistent to your ear. That's a sign of good writing.

Miss Understanding

Finish the story. Start with: *The librarian, named Miss Understanding, opened a can of worms by ...*

TAKE THE NEXT STEP

Readers understand more when you show instead of tell. Tell example: *My brother is funny and smart.* Show example: *My brother had the crowd in stitches as he sang the periodic table a la Frank Sinatra.* Turn this Tell into a Show: He was tired and happy.

DAY**90**

NAMING NAMES 1

Finish all four of these shorts. The starter will stay constant but your name will change.

Your name is Celeste. Start with: *He told me …*

_____

_____

_____

Your name is Bertha. Start with: *He told me …*

_____

_____

_____

Your name is Hank. Start with: *He told me …*

_____

_____

Your name is Percy. Start with: *He told me …*

_____

_____

_____

TAKE THE NEXT STEP

Circle one name that most appeals to you: Acel; Bewn; Copi; Dova; Ekna; Flyt; Gerf; Hasz; Itan; Julp; Karn; Loli; Meln; Nant; Ompa; Pury; Quij; Rolt; Sanu; Truf; Urat; Vran; Weqy; Xply; Yfra; Zigp. If this is now your name, how might your writing be different?

Tomorrow, write as if you are this person.

April Fools

The greatest practical joke I ever played used a computer shareware software program called LAVA which turned the monitor into a series of oozing and flowing colors. I installed it on a technophobic friend's brand new, first-ever computer. You should have seen the look of terror on his face! Write about a prank you've pulled or one that someone has pulled on you.

TAKE THE NEXT STEP

List six pranks or other April memories from your life.

Use these to prompt further writings.

DAY**92**

APE-X

You are a lemur who has escaped from your zoo display cage, only to find yourself in the ape house. Start with: *The diamond ...*

_____

_____

_____

_____

_____

TAKE THE NEXT STEP

Lemurs cling to tree limbs. When you cling to safe topics, your writing will often bore your reader. What's a topic that would be a bit scary for you to write?

Write on this topic NOW.

Superstitious

Start with: Whenever the phone rings ...

Use all these superstitions:

* If a bee enters your home, it's a sign that you will soon have a visitor. If you kill the bee, the visitor will be unpleasant.
* Touch blue, and your wish will come true.
* If your right ear itches, someone is speaking well of you.

TAKE THE NEXT STEP

You pick up the phone and a (living) writer you admire is on the other end. What would you say to get him or her to want to read something you've written? Put this in a note, find the writer's contact info, send it, and then forget about it.

Three Wishes

Fill the page. Start with: *He wished he …*

┌─◯
| **TAKE THE NEXT STEP**
|
| My mother-in-law (who I never met) was known to say, "Wish in
| one hand, poop in the other. See which you get first." Take an action
| today to turn a wish into a reality. Write the wish down. Write what
| action you will take to make it happen. *Now do it!*
└

Where have you been???

Use these four words:
Yellow · Iris · Quote · Joke

Start with: **"Where have you been?"**
she demanded. He dropped his eyes and ...

TAKE THE NEXT STEP

Do you drop your eyes when people ask about your
current writing? Practice so you can answer with confidence next time—while looking the asker in the eye.

Daydreamer

Finish the story.   Start with: *While the teacher lectured, I stared out the window ...*

_____

_____

_____

_____

_____

_____

_____

_____

_____

_____

_____

_____

_____

_____

TAKE THE NEXT STEP

Describe a window you remember using to daydream. Not the view; the actual window.

Now imagine you are there and daydream and stare out that mind window for a few minutes. What did you dream?

SCARRED STIFF

Finish the story. Start with: He had a scar ...

TAKE THE NEXT STEP

We all have emotional scars that keep us from writing what we want. Describe one of your scars as if it were a physical scar that you can actually see. Personify it. *Did anything change for you?*

PLACE-A-PERSONAL

Write the name of a place with which you are familiar, but not too familiar. Perhaps you drive by it or through it often, or have spent a day there, or a vacation.

[   ]

Now write something personal about yourself in the context of this place. If this exercise seems vague, you're right! Just go with it! Start with:

The one thing I know for sure about [   ] is ...

TAKE THE NEXT STEP

Describe the place where you are now writing as if it were a person. Include your relationship to this person-place.

If it's a good relationship, return here often to write. If not, keep choosing places to write until one works.

Un-Moral *one*

Use the un-moral at the bottom of the page to conclude the story you are about to write. Start with: *She was not a ...*

TAKE THE NEXT STEP

Count up all you've written in the last week (use whatever works best: word count, number of pages, hours spent writing, etc.) Your number: _____.

Set a new quantifiable writing goal for next week: _____.

Check back at the end of the week and applaud yourself, whether you achieved it or not. Setting a goal is a big accomplishment in and of itself.

THE UN-MORAL:
It's best to count your chickens before they're hatched.

Quack?

Write down six animal sounds, like MOO, BAA, QUACK, etc.

_____ _____ _____

_____ _____ _____

Use as many of these sounds as you can in a story starting with:
Some relationships are better than others ...

TAKE THE NEXT STEP

In order to not ruin a relationship when asked to critique someone's
writing, always offer specific constructive advice for each critique
you address. Practice by critiquing one specific thing on this page.

Now offer yourself a constructive way to change it.

DAY**101**

paint the town pink

Use the starting phrase and fill the page. Start with:

When I am in a neon pink mood ...

TAKE THE NEXT STEP

Now get out a red (or neon pink) pen and, using proof-reader's marks, mark up this page.

DAY **102**

Chip Off The Old Block

You are an alien who has been sent to earth. You arrive in the heart of New York City and land in the middle of a city block. The first thing you encounter is an unidentifiable object (known to earthlings as a melting chocolate chip.) Study it. Send a transmission back to your planet about your first earthly discovery!

Start with: *We have met our first ...*

TAKE THE NEXT STEP

Describe your writer-self in terms of being a chip. Are you a chocolate chip, potato chip, ice chip, or some other chip? Why? What can you do to make your chip more chipper? *Try it!*

News-Y Twos-Y

Walter Cronkite always signed off his newscast
with the line, "And that's the way it is."

Use this quote two times in this writing exercise.
Start with: *He worked up a good lather* …

TAKE THE NEXT STEP

Jot down four stories you've heard or seen in the news that
would make good starting points for stories or articles.

Next time you need something to write, use one of these.

DAY **104**

animal tendencies

TAKE THE NEXT STEP

When you are writing in flow, to which animal are you most similar? What are the traits? Keep a picture of this animal handy. Looking at it before you write will help you get into flow faster. Looking at it during writing will help you get back into the flow of things.

Think of an animal that you relate to. Use mental images of this animal throughout this exercise. Then fill in the blanks to create a piece of poetic prose.

The animal inside me wears _____
S/he is afraid of _____
And eats only _____

The animal inside me despises _____
S/he lives in _____
And plays with _____

The animal inside me sings _____
S/he has a collection of_____
And revels in _____

The animal inside me loves _____
S/he is waiting for _____
And wishes that _____
And sometimes when no one is looking, the animal inside me _____
_____

Apples to Oranges

Start with the word Apples and write a story or poem, using each letter as you get to it!

Apples_____ B_____
_____ C_____ D_____
_____ E_____ F_____
_____ G_____ H_____
_____ I_____ J_____
_____ K_____ L_____
_____ M_____ N_____
_____ O_____
P_____ Q_____
___ R_____ S_____
_____ T_____ U_____
_____ V_____ W_____
_____ X_____ Y_____
_____ Z_____.

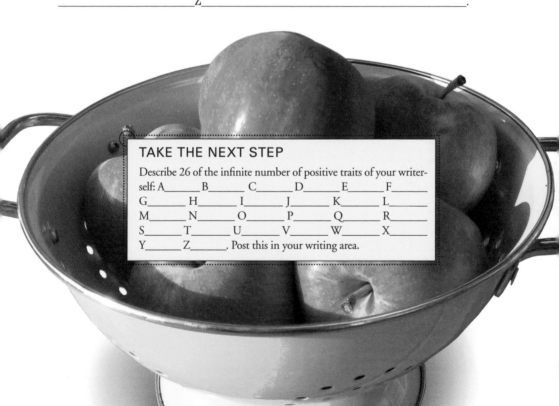

TAKE THE NEXT STEP

Describe 26 of the infinite number of positive traits of your writer-self: A_____ B_____ C_____ D_____ E_____ F_____
G_____ H_____ I_____ J_____ K_____ L_____
M_____ N_____ O_____ P_____ Q_____ R_____
S_____ T_____ U_____ V_____ W_____ X_____
Y_____ Z_____. Post this in your writing area.

S₁ C₂ R₁ I₁ B₃ B₃ L₂ E₁

This exercise uses letter tiles like a familiar word game. When you get to a letter and use it as the first letter of a word, you get two points. Try for 100 points!

My teeth …

_____ A₁ _____ R₁ _____

D₂ _____ I₁ _____ A₁ _____

_____ R₁ _____ R₁ _____ O₁ _____

_____ Y₄ _____ H₄ _____

_____ G₂ _____ V₄ _____

___ E₁ _____ Q₁₀ _____

_____ E₁ _____ N₁ _____

M₃ _____ M₃ _____ I₁ _____

_____ O₁ _____ E₁ _____ E₁ _____

___ O₁ _____ U₁ _____ A₁ _____ R₁ ____

_____ X₈ _____ A₁ _____

_____ U₁ _____ L₂ _____ L₂ _____

_____ T₁ _____ B₃ _____ I₁ ____

_____ B₃ _____ U₁ _____

_____ O₁ _____ A₁ _____ C₃ __

_____ E₁ _____ T₁ _____ A₁ _____

C₃ _____ E₁ _____ E₁ _____

_____ A₁ _____ I₁ _____

_____ K₅ _____ Y₄ _____

_____ F₄ _____

S₁ _____

H₄ _____ G₂ _____

_____ N₁ _____ U₁ _____

_____ D₂ _____

TAKE THE NEXT STEP

This book is like an artist's sketchbook—a perfect place for scribbles (free writing). Sometimes artists' sketches are shown in museums/galleries. Circle one part of today's writing that is "suitable for framing" because it shows off your natural writing talents. There's at least one gem on every page. Go back through this book and see for yourself.

YOUR SCORE:

DAY 107

DANCE LESSONS

Finish this sentence and then use the entire sentence in your story.

It's like _____,
which is how I feel about
going to the ballet.

Start with: *Sometimes it takes more than once for me to learn a lesson …*

TAKE THE NEXT STEP

When writing, you and your pen are really dancing on paper. Describe an experience
where the pen took the lead and you merely followed. (Make one up if necessary.)

re-STORE

Take a mental visit to your favorite childhood store.
Start with: The funny thing about ...

TAKE THE NEXT STEP

In my youth, my friends and I once pretended to case out the local 5&10 store for a major break-in. What area of writing would you like to break in to? What's stopping you? Do something today towards this break-in!

DAY **109**

Petite Paragraphs

ONE

Here is a chance to write short paragraphs of
memory snippets. Use the starters provided.

I remember throwing …

I remember when my best friend …

I remember Halloween …

I remember my first sip of …

I remember hitting …

I remember riding …

TAKE THE NEXT STEP
Very often in writing it is difficult
to find a common thread to tie all
the pieces together. Find three
threads to turn these six paragraphs into one piece of writing.
Dig beneath the obvious.

CARD TRICKS

Use all these in a story: **Queen of Hearts   Full Deck   Joker   Deal**

Start with: **The nastiest trick ever played ...**

TAKE THE NEXT STEP

Make up business cards on your computer with all your contact info identifying yourself as a writer. You'll look and feel professional. And you'll be taken more seriously.

SPRING
IN MY STEP

Finish the story.

It was a sunny May morning when I awoke with a special spring in my step. Somehow, overnight, I had merged with a slinky and was able to do all sorts of things other humans could not. For instance, when I …

TAKE THE NEXT STEP

For writers, spring is the perfect time to write Christmas, Hanukkah and New Years articles for magazines, since they run 4-6 months in advance. Jot some article ideas for publication two seasons from now.

Write one!

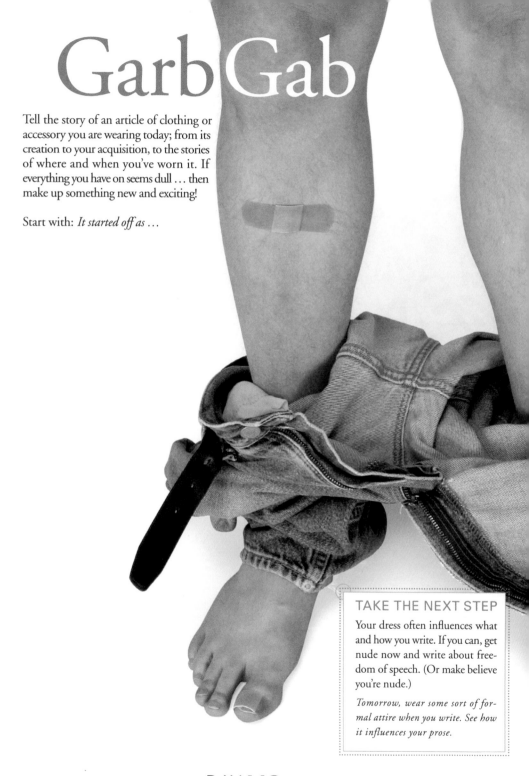

Garb Gab

Tell the story of an article of clothing or accessory you are wearing today; from its creation to your acquisition, to the stories of where and when you've worn it. If everything you have on seems dull ... then make up something new and exciting!

Start with: *It started off as ...*

TAKE THE NEXT STEP

Your dress often influences what and how you write. If you can, get nude now and write about freedom of speech. (Or make believe you're nude.)

Tomorrow, wear some sort of formal attire when you write. See how it influences your prose.

AMBIGUOUS

Use this ambiguous sentence in a story:

Mary was cooking in the pot.

Start with:

I could have used a kick in the seat of the pants the day that ...

TAKE THE NEXT STEP

Make believe your writing is something you cooked. Write a rave review for it like a food/restaurant critic would.

Use this as a motivational kick in the pants the next time your writing practice wanes.

LOOK MA... TWO HANDS!

Quick! Go get a second writing implement. For this exercise, you are going to write with both hands at the same time. To make it a little easier on you and your brain, you'll be using the same starting phrase and writing the same words (while you use both hands at the same time!!)

On this side of the page,
Write with your LEFT hand:

When the hot air balloon...

On this side,
Use your RIGHT hand:

When the hot air balloon ...

TAKE THE NEXT STEP

Imagine shaking hands with your first or next publisher. What does he or she see in your eyes?

TAKE THE NEXT STEP

What does writing success smell like to you? Be very specific. Get something (legal) that reminds you of this smell and inhale it often!

Nose-y

Write a smell you love here.

Now write a story incorporating this smell,

starting with: When I was ...

(Now think of a smell you hate, and finish your story incorporating this smell.)

DAY **116**

Happy Husband

First, fill in the blanks with appropriate words, then write the story using the words. Start with:

Whenever my wife *active verb: _____ ,
I want to *active verb: _____ into a …

TAKE THE NEXT STEP

We all see ourselves different-ly than others see us. Think of your biggest fan and describe yourself as a writer through this per-son's eyes and heart.

Take it in. It's true.

* a bathroom item:
* feminine item:

* a color:
* a texture:

* a place:
* item from a sport:

Pick an Age (circle one)
BETWEEN:
18 · 19 · 20 · 21 · 22 · 23 · 24 · 25 · 26 · 27 · 28

SETTING:
• name of a city/town
• Type of residency (or)

{ ← HOUSE ⌂ }

choose a → prominent Physical Feature:

Pick an eye color: _____

PICK A HAIR COLOR

CREATE A NAME
FIRST NAME STARTING WITH R, LAST NAME STARTING WITH G

MR R

a PASSION G

WHAT A CHARACTER!

You are now officially this character. Write starting with:
I thought I had been asking politely, but obviously ... _____
_____
_____
_____
_____
_____
_____
_____
_____
_____
_____
_____
_____
_____

TAKE THE NEXT STEP

Dialogue is a great way to start a story. Imagine two airport baggage claim attendants are your characters. Set a ten minute timer and let the characters talk.

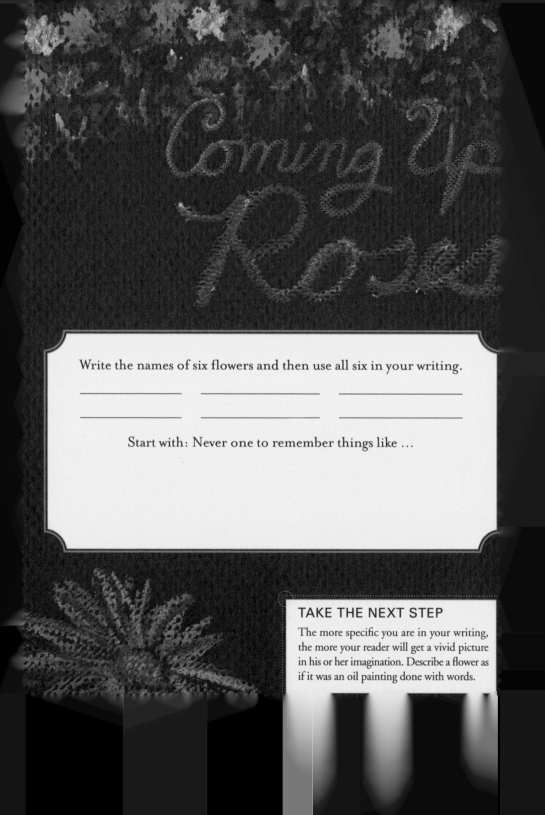

Write the names of six flowers and then use all six in your writing.

_____   _____   _____

_____   _____   _____

Start with: Never one to remember things like …

TAKE THE NEXT STEP

The more specific you are in your writing, the more your reader will get a vivid picture in his or her imagination. Describe a flower as if it was an oil painting done with words.

The Journalist & The Journaler

You are a 21-year old young woman from Germany about to marry an American journalist. The wedding is in two hours. You have been a devout journal keeper your whole life. Write your last entry as a single woman.

Start with: *The clock in this room …*

TAKE THE NEXT STEP

Clocks tell more than time. Describe three clocks from your life.

1.

2.

3.

Give these descriptions a permanent home by dropping them directly into future writings.

SPRING FORWARD

Finish the story. Start with:
**SOMETIMES
YOU JUST HAVE TO TAKE
A LEAP OF FAITH …**

TAKE THE NEXT STEP

Sending your writing out into the world requires a leap of faith in yourself. Write about what your life will be like if you DON'T ever take the leap and send out your writing.

Time to take the leap and do it!

Giraffe DODGER!

You are a giraffe in the zoo who has a crush on a woman in a maid's uniform who visits you every Thursday at noon. Start with: *She brought me ...*

She brought me...

TAKE THE NEXT STEP

There's a goldfish in a bowl next to you. You are his only entertainment. From his point of view, describe what he enjoys about your quirks, your writing habits, etc.

In order to not deprive him his entertainment, write every day!

DAY **122**

Double or Nothing

Write using the starter. Whatever word it is that you write when you come to the first double part of the line, you must use that same word every time you come to another double line on the rest of the page!

Start with: He said, "Double or nothing?" And I answered ...

_____

_____

_____

_____

_____

_____

_____

_____

_____

_____

TAKE THE NEXT STEP

I dare you to double your productivity right now and do another page in this book. Then take off tomorrow. See if you feel different—on the double day as compared to the off day. Remember, a day off doesn't mean you are quitting. You're simply recharging your batteries, a necessary part of being a good writer.

_____

_____

DAY 123

Kite Fight

Fill in the two shapes using the starters provided. Try to make your short pieces oppose and contrast one another … a genuine kite fight!

He landed …

He flew …

TAKE THE NEXT STEP

You are the best person to promote your own writing. In essence, you have to fly your own kite for all to see. Write a catchy headline for a press release to the major media about you and your writing.

DAY **124**

famous firsts {two}

Finish the story.

Start with: The patient, an old-fashioned man, thought the nurse made a mistake in keeping both of the windows open, and her sprightly disregard of his protests added something to his hatred of her.

(This first line is from Alice Adams by Booth Tarkington.)

TAKE THE NEXT STEP

Which one writer would you like to invite to a dinner party? What's the one question about writing practice or process you'd like to ask him or her? He or she has thrown this question back at you. What's your answer?

YOU ARE A 58-YEAR OLD

NURSE WHO IS A

HYPOCHONDRIAC AND

WORKS IN AN ALLER-

GIST'S OFFICE. WRITE

FROM THIS PERSPECTIVE.

START WITH: I HUNG UP

ON HIM TWICE …

Hang Ups

TAKE THE NEXT STEP

We all have hang ups about something we do poorly in the writing craft. List two of yours:

1.
2.

Now go find a book or information on the Internet to help you improve in these areas and develop more confidence.

DAY **126**

Silent Treatment

Finish the story. Start with: *We sat in silence for …*

⊕··
: **TAKE THE NEXT STEP**
:
: Very often when someone critiques us, we remain
: silent (intentionally or unintentionally). Here's a chance
: to tell off one of those critiquers. Go to town!
··

DAY **127**

CLOSED
ENCOUNTERS

>─┤─◆>─◍─<◆>─┤─<◇>─┤─◆>─◍─<◆>─┤─<◇>─┤─◆>─◍─<◆>─┤─<

You are now going to write with your eyes closed. You may find
it helpful to use your other hand to support/guide your movement down the page. There are no lines on the page to make it
easier for you. Start with: *I don't see why ...*

TAKE THE NEXT STEP

Name one facet of your writing for which you'd like to seek support.

What is keeping you from asking for help?

Debunk the reasoning behind not asking.

Now go ahead and ask for that help or support.

Closed Encounters – The Sequel

Now that you have survived writing with your eyes closed, you are now going to write with your eyes closed using your non-dominant hand. You may find it helpful once again to use your dominant hand to guide your movement down the page. There are no lines on the page to make it easier for you. Start with: *Every time I see …*

TAKE THE NEXT STEP

Sometimes when we're in the thick of writing a long work, the middle gets muddy and we can't see our way out. The middle can have just as much energy as the beginning or end. Like Oreo cookies, think of other wonderful middles and compare them to your writing process.

QUESTIONS-ONE

Answer the 20 questions by circling one option.
When done you'll have a character sketch.

You are this person.
Write from their perspective.
Start with:

The stars were so bright that night …

Film strip questions:

YOUNG OR OLD

ORGANIZED OR CHAOTIC

TALL OR SHORT

THIN LIPS OR THICK LIPS

SENSITIVE OR CALLOUS

BLUE EYES OR BROWN EYES

MALE OR FEMALE

GREEN THUMB OR KILLS CACTI

THIN OR FAT

ACTIVE OR SEDENTARY

SOFT SPOKEN OR ABRUPT

WIDE NOSE OR SKI SLOPE NOSE

SMOKER OR NON-SMOKER

BIG EARS OR TINY EARS

DOGS OR CATS

FAIR OR DARK HAIRED

VANILLA OR CHOCOLATE CAKE

NAIL BITER OR WELL MANICURED

HONEST OR DISHONEST

SMILING OR GRIMACING

TAKE THE NEXT STEP

You have written a book titled *Bright Star.*
Your publisher has just requested a brief bio
for the back cover. Compose it.

Idioms Delight — two

Start with the idiom: *He always has a bone to pick ...*

Use the idiomatic expression, *I haven't scratched the surface,* in your conclusion.

TAKE THE NEXT STEP

Sometimes picking just one thing to write about feels like you're missing out on lots of other options. By not choosing, you're missing out on the joy of committing to, following through on, and completing something. Choose one writing project to commit to now.

Keep a list of the other topics for the future.

france with no pants

You have just won a free two-day trip to France. There's a catch. You must leave immediately. There's no time to go home and pack. All you can bring is what you are wearing and carrying with you today. Plus, you are given 15 minutes and $25 to spend at an airport store. What do you buy, if anything?

Tell the story of your adventure to the person sitting next to you on the flight home. Start with: *What a whirlwind …*

TAKE THE NEXT STEP

Many writers are adrenaline junkies, only able to create when pressure is on or the muse is screaming in their ear. Where do you get your energy and motivation to write?

Is there something different you'd like to try? Like what?

Snapshots 2

Photos are a great way to capture memories. But we don't always have a camera with us. Write quick "word snapshots" as substitutes for the following topics. Try to capture colors, textures, and expressions. Use your own life story ... or make it up!

A city vacation ...

Children playing ...

Dancing ...

A war ...

TAKE THE NEXT STEP
List six snapshots from your life that took place in May.

Use these to prompt further writings.

FOR WHOM THE BELL
TOLLS

Finish the story. Start with: The factory bell ...

TAKE THE NEXT STEP

A bell rings to signal the end of the workday. If you had all the freedom in the world, how would you spend your free evening? Go there in your mind.

Writing is a great escape that takes you places you wouldn't otherwise go for an evening.

Sideways Glance

Sometimes writing in a different direction changes how you write. Try it! Start with:
I couldn't help staring ...

TAKE THE NEXT STEP

Stretch your peripheral vision by looking as far to the right and left as you can without moving your head. Describe what might be right beyond what you see.

Stretching our eyes, minds, legs, and hearts is very helpful to developing writing muscle!

Flipper - One

Below are four backwards words. When you get to each word, flip them in your mind so they become real words. Use that word in your story, before you get to the next word. (Don't read the words first—that spoils the fun!) Start with, *I remember laughing …*

DRIB

LIAN

KNIP

EPAC

TAKE THE NEXT STEP

A comedy writing rule of thumb is to use lots of K sounds because they are naturally funnier than other sounds. Just saying K makes your mouth smile. Form a list of K words for future reference. Here's a start: *Pickle, Turkey, Cucumber, Alka Seltzer …*

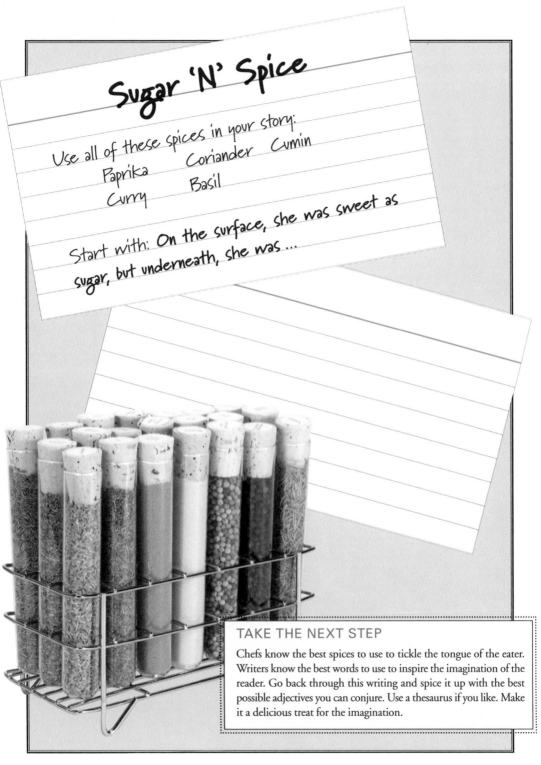

Sugar 'N' Spice

Use all of these spices in your story:
Paprika   Coriander   Cumin
Curry   Basil

Start with: On the surface, she was sweet as sugar, but underneath, she was ...

TAKE THE NEXT STEP

Chefs know the best spices to use to tickle the tongue of the eater. Writers know the best words to use to inspire the imagination of the reader. Go back through this writing and spice it up with the best possible adjectives you can conjure. Use a thesaurus if you like. Make it a delicious treat for the imagination.

Hit A Homer

Use each letter as you get to it in your story.
Start with: *The yo-yo fad was in full swing when …*

H
  O
    M
      E
        R
          H
            O
              M
                E
                  R
                    H
                      O
                        M
                          E
                            R

TAKE THE NEXT STEP

When your writing elevator gets stuck, which floor (or between which floors) of a 100-floor building are you usually on?

Don't worry about getting right to the penthouse suite, just concentrate on getting to the next floor. What's one thing you can do to get up to the next floor now? Write floor by floor.

Make Believe

Finish the story. Start with: *I used to pretend …*

TAKE THE NEXT STEP

Pretend you are an archaeologist digging up feelings from when you were three years old. What do you find? Where do you find them? How can you incorporate these into your current writing?

DAY **139**

BATHROOM HUMOR

When I run workshops, we go around the circle and introduce ourselves. Introductions are almost never about writing. Some examples are: favorite Halloween costume, what you eat for breakfast, how many times you re-set the snooze alarm. The most humorous of all topics was sparked by a most untidy restroom in the bookstore where we were meeting: "Describe your favorite public restroom … and if you don't have one, describe your least favorite." Time for you to do the same … NOW!

TAKE THE NEXT STEP

Take this book with you into the bathroom and stand in the shower or tub. Shout "I am a writer" out loud five times.

Describe a time in your past that this moment triggers.

Do this in other places and then write the memories.

un MORAL 2

Use the un-moral at the bottom of the page to conclude the story you are about to write.
Start with: *The beads of sweat ...*

And the un-moral of the story is:
Every clown has a silver lining.

TAKE THE NEXT STEP

Describe some tears that your inner clown wanted to cry but didn't or couldn't.

Use these feelings next time you sit down to write.

DAY **141**

Walk In The Park – One

You are out walking. Two joggers pass you. You overhear a tiny tidbit of their conversation: "… And the explosion was so …" You are certain this is what you heard. Imagine on paper what it is they were talking about. (Or continue their conversation in dialogue format.)

TAKE THE NEXT STEP

There's no such thing as an overnight success. You're on a talk show now and have been asked to describe the major events that led up to when you exploded onto the writing scene.

FOOTSIES

Finish the story. Start with: *Painted toenails always …*

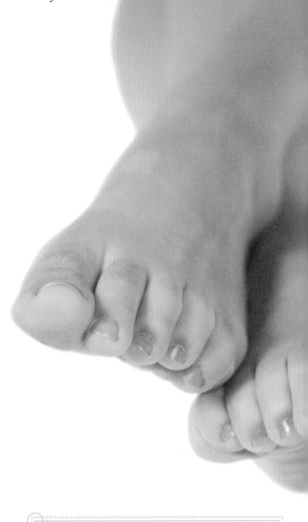

TAKE THE NEXT STEP

Without looking down, describe what, if your feet had eyes, they'd see right now.

Writing practice combines your power of observation and your power of imagination.

BUBBLE RAP—TWO

Create a dialogue between two people, using the speech bubbles provided.
There are two shapes, one per person. There is a starter to get you on your way.

Come here often?

TAKE THE NEXT STEP

Imagine this shape is you: ○

And this shape is your writing practice: □

Draw a representation of how they combine
in your life. Examples: ○□ ○ ○

Don't Sweat It

Finish the story. Start with: *If I weren't allergic to sweating, I'd ...*

TAKE THE NEXT STEP

If you could plant one seed for your writing future,
what would you want it to grow to be?

Do one thing today to nurture this seed.

DAY **145**

What I Did on My Summer Vacation

The classic assignment! Start with the given letter and fill in each line with something you have done on summer vacations. Focus on one year or many years. Example: Ate overripe plums that dripped down my arms while I drove through Amish farm country. Have fun! The odder and stranger the entries, the better!!

A_____
B_____
C_____
D_____
E_____
F_____
G_____
H_____
I_____
J_____
K_____
L_____
M_____
N_____

O_____
P_____
Q_____
R_____
S_____
T_____
U_____
V_____
W_____
X_____
Y_____
Z_____

TAKE THE NEXT STEP

Just like a photographer shooting a roll of film, when it comes to writing, "summer better than others." Go back through this writing and pick the one item that's the best shot in the roll. Circle it. Why did you pick this one?

KEYED UP

Use all
these words.
Start with:

While surfing the Web ...

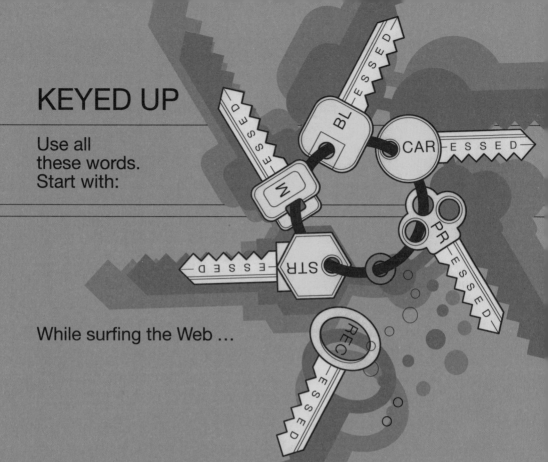

TAKE THE NEXT STEP

Describe a person you know who does everything slowly and methodically. Write at their slow speed. If this describes you, write about yourself, but write really fast.

Try a new pace next time you write.

Numb Numbers

wherever you come to a number on the page, use it in your story. Start with: while waiting, I ...

4

222

3,142

16

0

771

TAKE THE NEXT STEP

On a 1–100% scale of currently available time that you could be using to write, what percent of this time do you actually spend writing? What non-writing thing could you do less of to bring this writing percent up a couple percentage points? *Try it and see what happens.*

Lessons Learned

Write about a teacher or mentor you've had. Use as many adjectives and descriptive phrases as you can—to excess, even! Start with:

Most teachers have eyes in the back of their heads, but ...

TAKE THE NEXT STEP

There's a lesson in everything, including regrets. List one regret you have in the area of writing. Now turn this into a positive lesson by focusing on one positive facet: *I am proud of…*

TAKE THE NEXT STEP

There are a million ways to show characters' emotions. Practice with these:

Nurse/Pride

Beautician/Dread

Custodian/Jealousy

Write three action words/verbs:

_____
_____
_____

Write three descriptive words/adjectives:

_____
_____
_____

Use them ALL in a story. Start with:
If I've told you once, I've told you a million times ...

@#$%
*?#!$@!!!!

I've told you
a million times!

DAY **150**

Fictionary Two

Write a dictionary-style definition for CINCHONISM, pronounced SING ke NIZ um.

Use CINCHONISM with your fictitious definition in a story. Start with: *The stars were …*

TAKE THE NEXT STEP

Writing is not just output. It's also input. Have you ever been to an observatory, gone skydiving, or spoken in front of 1,000 people? List things you'd like to experience.

Schedule one now for the sake of your craft.

Star, all-star constellation
star-spangled
applications
including
intelligent
important
less-than-perfect
abound.
nutrients
features
, would sick, from the
big and small
your eyes but By Order
only the silly things
, assets probably highest
prospects don't Their
ingredients favorite
rolled magic dragon scale
If you quality more
we put unique notice
be yanked increase safe
available because
That's Honorable likely.

The real definition of cinchonism: *a pathological condition resulting from an overdose of cinchona bark, a tree/shrub native to the Andes whose bark yields quinine.* How close was your definition?

INITIAL INITIALS

Use your first and last initials to generate the components to make up this story.

	Beginning with your first initial	Beginning with your last initial
Body of water		
Flower		
Food		
First name		
Last name		

You now have two characters and a bunch of words to be used creatively! For example: If your flower is Petunia, use it as a nickname. If your food is Fruit Loops, use it for someone's state of mind! If your water is Babbling Brook, use it in a metaphor. Write about these two characters, starting with:

Sometimes things just ...

_____

_____

_____

_____

_____

_____

_____

_____

TAKE THE NEXT STEP

What was the initial spark that got you to creatively put pen to paper?

Now that you've recaptured it, what can you do to keep that initial spark alive every time you sit down to write?

DAY **152**

You are a groundskeeper who talks to all your plants.

You believe that talking to them is better than talking to friends about your problems, and definitely better than talking to a therapist.

One tree, a Juniper, who you have named JUNE, is your favorite.

Start with: Can you believe it? She called me again last night...

JUNE

THE JUNIPER

TAKE THE NEXT STEP

Confide six memories that took place in your life in June.

Use these to prompt further writing.

Gems

Use the words as you get to them. Start with: *I plucked the _____ from …*

sparkling sapphire

blinded by a diamond

ruby red

aquamarine

precious

black pearls

TAKE THE NEXT STEP

Unusual sensory combinations spark readers' imaginations and send them to places they normally wouldn't go on their own. Here are two: the smell of a joke, the taste of a territory. Come up with some of your own to use in future writings.

PICK ♣ SIX

Without moving, write down six things within your line of vision: they can be actions, people, items, textures, or emotions:

THING ONE

THING TWO

THING THREE

THING FOUR

THING FIVE

THING SIX

Now use all six of these in a piece that begins: It's funny, the more I …

TAKE THE NEXT STEP

Point of view influences a story. Go back and change this one from first person (I, we) to third person (he, she, it, they). Do you think you'll only change pronouns? What other changes do you expect to make? *Now do it. What surprised you?*

Ambidextrous

Use your least dominant hand to write this exercise. Even if it feels odd and uncomfortable, STICK WITH IT! The lines are spread out to help you. Start with: *I remember my first …*

TAKE THE NEXT STEP

What was the first compliment you remember receiving about your writing? From whom? Do you remember what you had written? How did it affect your future writings?

GIFTED

Finish the story. Start with: *Here's a photo from my second birthday, where I preferred the wrapping paper over the ...*

TAKE THE NEXT STEP

Think out of the box and compare what you just wrote ...

... to a gift

... to being 16

... to a kumquat

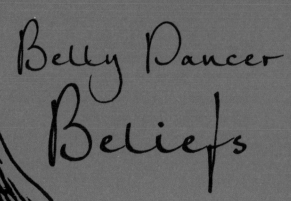

Belly Dancer Beliefs

You are a belly dancer. Complete each of these four shorts in her voice.

Guns are …

The right to …

Stephen King is …

Republicans are …

TAKE THE NEXT STEP

Where do your characters come from? Combine two people you know—one relative and one friend—to come up with a new character. *Next time you write, use this character's point of view.*

WEIRD WORDS -2-

Use the words CEDI, EKPWELE, KWACHA, and OUGUIYA in your story—even though you probably don't know what they mean. Set your story in New York City at the height of a summer heat wave. Start with: The layers of …

TAKE THE NEXT STEP

What items, behaviors, circumstances, atmospheres, chores do you think are necessary to be in place before you sit down to write?

Choose one that you are willing to give up tomorrow. Try it and see what happens!

(These words are international currency: CEDI - Ghana, EKPWELE - Equatorial Guinea, KWACHA - Zambia, OUGUIYA - Mauritania)

Tooth Fairy

You are a disgruntled Tooth Fairy. You can't understand why Santa and even the Easter Bunny get more attention than you. You just visited twins who expected $20 per tooth. Start with:

I can't believe ...

TAKE THE NEXT STEP

Characters often live beyond one piece of writing. Write something that will happen in the future to one of the characters in this story as a result of this writing.

Do this a with character that has stuck with you from another writing.

EST

Use all these words.

MANIFEST

JEST

PROTEST

ZEST

Start with: Back in the sixties, or maybe it was already the seventies by then ...

TAKE THE NEXT STEP

Here's a TEST for you. With ZEST, go back through this page of writing and figure out the BEST place to really start the story. Then number your sentences or paragraphs to reorder the REST of the tale. LEST you leave anything that is superfluous, cross out all that is not vital or necessary to the story. I can be a real PEST, can't I?

Cheery *Cherry*

Think about a cherry ... the feel, smell, taste, color.
Write three memories or impressions that come to mind.

Now use these three in a story.
Start with: *Her cheeriness makes me ...*

TAKE THE NEXT STEP

Which one or two of your senses do you use most often in your writing?
Which do you use least? Go back and add this sense to the story on this
page. (Do it twice!) Remember to use it in your future writings as well.

DAY **162**

Here Ye

Start with: Here ye sits and thinks if only ye had something to write, ye would be in a state of delight.
And so ye begins, with a dip of the quill …

TAKE THE NEXT STEP

Describe a time when you thought you had nothing to write,
weren't in the mood to write, or your muse was in hiding, yet
you were very prolific.

Remember this the next time you think you've got writer's block.

DAY **163**

Body Talk

You're a recently divorced, middle-aged woman. Today you went to a psychic to find out what is in your future. You have just returned home. And you phone your best friend. You get an answering machine. Leave a long message covering all the details (good and bad.) Use these nine words:

deFEAT   HANDy   drIES
gEARS   BesTOWS   sTUNG
NOSEy   SHINdig   NEEdle

Start with: *You'll never believe what the psychic said!*
The next time there is snow ...

TAKE THE NEXT STEP

Listen and your ears will tell you what you don't hear as well as what you do hear. Have you ever heard the silence of snow? Try to capture the sound of sunshine.

Made-up Words – One

Connect these prefixes, roots and suffices as you like to come up with four made-up words.

PREFIX		ROOT		SUFFIX
RE		*splitter*		ing
PRE	**+**	**PEPPER**	**+**	izer
UN		mimic		**ATHON**
dis		PHOTO		ator

Your made-up words:

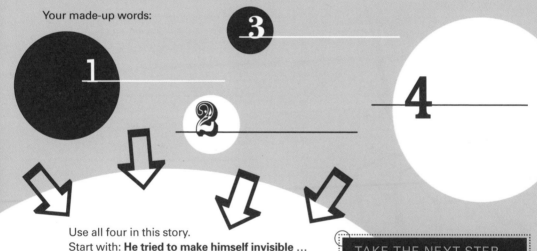

3 _____

1 _____

2 _____

4 _____

Use all four in this story.
Start with: **He tried to make himself invisible …**

TAKE THE NEXT STEP

Combine these jumbled prefixes, roots, and suffices to create a word that positively describes your writing process.

Pro; Super; Sym; Comp; Form; Styl; Spin; Tale; Flow; Mus; Word; Izer; Ing; Ator; Aptor.

Write a definition for the word.

Hang it on your wall and look at it often!

DAY **165**

Gymnastics

Use the given letter to begin each line of your story.
Start with: *On my way to the gym ...*

G _____
y _____
M _____
G _____
y _____
M _____
G _____
y _____
M _____.
G _____
y _____
M _____
G _____
y _____
M _____
G _____
y _____
M _____
G _____
y _____
M _____
G _____
y _____
M _____

TAKE THE NEXT STEP

Olympic gymnasts have coaches who support them in
all their pursuits. Writers can set up a writing coaching
partnership. You and your partner help each other stay
on path for goals by asking questions. Here are some to
get you started: What is in my way that is keeping me
from accomplishing _____? Who put it there? Can
it be removed? How?

DAY **166**

SCRIBBLE - THREE

This exercise uses letter tiles like a familiar word game. When you get to a letter and use it as the first letter of a word, you get two points. Try for 100 points!

YOUR SCORE:_____

Being in limbo …

TAKE THE NEXT STEP

Describe a time when you felt very, very, very alive.
Use this feeling when you write next.

DAY **167**

Father & Son

You are a father who just discovered a major dent in your car. You approach your teenage son. Start with: *It has come to my attention …*

TAKE THE NEXT STEP

A great way to brainstorm a story is to start with a question such as:

What would life be like if _____?

What would happen if _____?

Fill in these blanks and then answer one, or create a question of your own and answer it. Do it in five minutes or less.

DAY**168**

SMELL A RAT

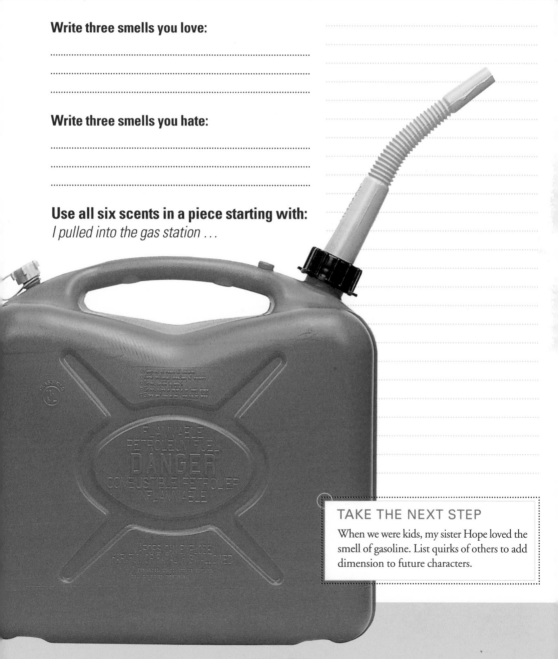

Write three smells you love:

....

....

....

Write three smells you hate:

....

....

....

Use all six scents in a piece starting with:
I pulled into the gas station . . .

TAKE THE NEXT STEP

When we were kids, my sister Hope loved the smell of gasoline. List quirks of others to add dimension to future characters.

Happy Endings — Two

Use the last sentence at the bottom of the
page to conclude your story.

Again he paced the floor, but his
path was not nine feet by two.

(Last sentence from *Ann Vickers* by Sinclair Lewis.)

TAKE THE NEXT STEP

Pacing yourself when writing a long piece is very helpful.
Describe how you can apply a pacing tool that benefited
you in another area of your life to your writing. *Try it!*

Time Warp

THINK OF AN ERA YOU WOULD LIKE TO BE FROM (PAST OR FUTURE). GIVE YOURSELF A NEW NAME FROM THIS TIME, USING YOUR CURRENT INITIALS. IF YOU THINK YOU ALSO SHOULD BE OF THE OPPOSITE SEX, MAKE THAT CHANGE TOO.

NAME:

RELIGION: CURRENT AGE:

WHAT DO YOU SPEND YOUR DAYS DOING?

WHO IS THE CLOSEST PERSON TO YOU?

WHAT IS YOUR FAVORITE POSSESSION?

YOU ARE NOW THIS CHARACTER. WRITE FROM HIS OR HER PERSPECTIVE. START WITH: IT WAS SO CLOSE I COULD TASTE IT ...

TAKE THE NEXT STEP

If you could travel back in time in your current life, what one writing moment would you relive? Why? *You just did. Hope you enjoyed it!*

PETITE PARAGRAPHS—TWO

Here is a chance to write short paragraphs of memory snippets. Use the starters provided.

I remember running ...

I remember spitting ...

I remember growing ...

I remember Valentine's Day ...

I remember liking ...

I remember feeling ...

TAKE THE NEXT STEP

Take one phrase from each of these six paragraphs and combine them to form a poem.

Cool, huh?

DAY **172**

Ode to a Season

Here's a chance to roast your least favorite season. Write in second tense (you). As an example, here is a first line about summer: *Although you are lauded by most, I despise your pea-soup breath that strangles like an assassin's noose.*

Ode to..

....

....

....

....

....

....

....

....

TAKE THE NEXT STEP

If your writing practice were a garden, what would it look like? Be honest! In keeping with the garden theme, what's one new way you can tend to your writing that you've never tried before? *Do it!*

FREE TO BEE

Start with the word BEE and free associate. Write down whatever comes to mind.

BEE

Circle eight interesting words. Use them in a story about a recently freed prisoner. Start with:

I have been ...

TAKE THE NEXT STEP

Write a story idea here. _____

Free associate ideas from it. _____

Did you find a topic you like better? _____

SQUARESVILLE

Start

Use the starter and then fill in
the squares as you see fit.
Be inventive!

*In the summer of '25 I led an excursion of
four men and four women through a …*

TAKE THE NEXT STEP

Have a writer's jam session by filling in this
area with words/phrases as you like:

How was it to start with a blank area?

End

DAY **175**

Pillow Talk

All pillows come with warning labels: Under penalty of law ... this tag not to be re-moved ... except by the consumer. Think of a favorite pillow or cushion. Write what the warning label should indicate. Example: Warning! Exercise extreme caution when thinking about this pillow while operating heavy machinery.

Now write a story and make reference to this pillow.
Start with: The salesperson was so ...

TAKE THE NEXT STEP

If your closest friends were asked if they think you come with warning labels, how would they respond? *Seeing yourself from different points of view makes writing about other people easier.*

UN-MORAL—THREE

Use the un-moral at the bottom of the page to conclude the story you are about to write. Start with: *The quick beating of ...*

And the un-moral is: You *can* make a silk purse out of a sow's ear.

TAKE THE NEXT STEP

Silk, satin and other sibilant S sounds and syllables seem to sensuously slide off the tongue. List more for the next time you have to set such a scene.

PHILLY PHONETICS

Whenever possible I like to put in a plug for my hometown, Philadelphia, PA.
Use these four linguistic gems from Philly in your story:

Youze (more than one person in the second person, as in *Where youze goin'?*)
Mayan (not yours, as in *Don't touch that, it's mayan!*)
Hoagie (submarine sandwich, as in *Gimme a hoagie wit da works!*)
Down D' Shore (New Jersey beach, as in *We left d'city early t'head down d'shore.*)

Start with: *We got two cheesesteaks t' go and …*_____

_____

_____

_____

_____

_____

_____

_____

_____

TAKE THE NEXT STEP
What foods from your area can
you mention in your writing to
add local flavor? Make a list for
future reference.

DAY **178**

NAME GAME

Tell the origin of your first name.
Were you named for someone?
Is it a name of your parents' own creation?
If you don't know, make it up ...
Also write interesting anecdotes about your last name.
Be as wild as you like.
Start with:
It was a difficult decision ...

TAKE THE NEXT STEP

Choose a pen name/nom de plume for yourself. Does having one free you to write new topics? Why or why not? Do you feel like you want to save your best stuff for your own name?

Curlers In Your Hair!

*List three famous people with naturally curly hair
(or curly tops in your life):*

*Use all three names in a story. Start with: It's been said that
blondes have more fun, but …*

TAKE THE NEXT STEP

What's one thing you do or wear that most people you know would consider
'out of character'? How can you incorporate this trait into something you're
currently writing? Or into your writing practice?

MUSE-INGS

A CHANCE TO INVITE YOUR MUSE FOR A VISIT! IF YOU DON'T BELIEVE YOU HAVE ONE, MAKE ONE UP! ANSWER THE QUESTIONS DIRECTLY IN THE SHAPES … DRAW IF YOU LIKE! HAVE FUN!

What does your muse walk like?

What does your muse sound like?

What does your muse do for fun?

What does your muse wear?

What does your muse smile like?

Where does your muse live?

What does your muse like to eat?

What does your muse smell like?

TAKE THE NEXT STEP

Write a thank you note from your muse to you.

Read it out loud so you can take in every word!

DAY **181**

Summer Better Than Others

Finish the story. *Even though he is my best friend, there are some things he says that drive me nuts. Every June 30th, when the year is half over, he always says, "Six of one, half dozen of another." It was clever when we were nine, but now it makes me want to …*

TAKE THE NEXT STEP

Think hard—What do you have six of, but only six? If you have nothing, make it up and then write a mini anecdote as to why you only have six.

Jewel   Eye   Fourth

Incorporate a lie or lye in this story.
Start with: July in the city is usually a time when ...

_____

_____

_____

_____

_____

_____

_____

_____

_____

_____

_____

_____

_____

TAKE THE NEXT STEP

List six lies or truths that took place in a July of your past.

Use these to prompt further writings.

DAY **183**

Time to write a story in bits and pieces. Hereafter, whenever you pick up this book, come back to this page. Today, start with the given starter and write until you get to the dot. Next time write until you get to the second dot … and so on. (There are sixteen dots!)

One day at a time

I remember that hairstyle …

DECEMBER 3

TAKE THE NEXT STEP

Not many people like their driver's license or school photos. Create a character sketch of someone who does. Incorporate this character into the next thing you write.

Dear Diary—2

Circle one age option:

99-yr. old woman   55-yr. old divorced man
36-yr. old bartender   43-yr. old astrologer
17-yr. old high school football player

Circle one location option:

Lives in Brussels   Lives in a hotel
Lives with two women   Lives on the bayou
Lives on the grounds of a resort

You are now this person and this is where you live. You just found a diary from 1492. Let the story unfold. Start with:

I expected to find ...

TAKE THE NEXT STEP

Columbus sailed the ocean blue in 1492. If you had lived in his time, would you have been an explorer? In what areas of your writing could you be more adventurous? *Pick one and explore it today.*

Rock & Roll

Finish the story. Start with: *He was a little bit rock & roll and a little bit …*

TAKE THE NEXT STEP

Even when you're stuck in traffic there are always creative writing exercises you can do! Think of the first line of a song you really like. Write new lyrics for second and third lines.

STATE FAIR

Finish the story. Start with:
The best summer of my life was the one when Aunt Nan
came to stay for three weeks and at the state fair my …

TAKE THE NEXT STEP

What's your relationship with your writing? Are you
a wicked stepmother, caring aunt, little brother, over-
protective father, or something else? Describe it. If
you'd prefer a different relationship, describe that one.
Now do something to nurture this new relationship.

OH NO!

Use the expressions as you get to them.
Start with: "Oh No!" Why …

NO DICE

NO PROBLEM

NO TIME LIKE THE PRESENT

NO NEWS IS GOOD NEWS

NO SWEAT

NO WAY

TAKE THE NEXT STEP

Next time you get a rejection or a critique, don't think, "Oh no!" Think the reverse: "On ho!" Write how you'll handle this scenario to immediately move forward.

DAY **188**

en-title-ment

Write the first titles that come to mind.

Titles of two books:

Titles of two songs:

Titles of two magazines:

Choose one of these as the title of your story and then use the other five in the content of what you write. They don't have to be used as literal titles at all. For example, if you chose the song "Leaving On A Jet Plane," you could use it as a phrase instead.

Your story title:

Visonary

Finish these shorts. Starters are provided.

He winked at me …

I blinked and …

She batted her eyes …

He was always squinting …

TAKE THE NEXT STEP

Visionaries see trends. Writers must also track trends to submit articles and book proposals. List three trends you now see from reading, observation, contact with youth, etc., that you would like to write about. *Tackle one!*

BANANAS

Think about a banana ... the feel, smell, taste, color.
Write three memories/impressions that come to mind.

1.

2.

3.

Now use these three in a story. Start with: *He was a really nice guy ...*

TAKE THE NEXT STEP

If "Nice guys finish last" is true ... What "nice guy"
trait of yours can you eliminate in order to get further
ahead in your writing? With this trait gone, what will
you do today to move your writing along?

VOCAL-EYES — ONE

Finish the story. Start with:

I met her voice before I met her eyes ...

TAKE THE NEXT STEP

Finding your writing voice is important. Pick two things you now see and write them down. Give each a voice and write in that voice, having them each describe how they see you.

VOCAL-EYES — TWO

FINISH THE STORY.

Start with: *I met his eye long before I heard that familiar voice ...*

TAKE THE NEXT STEP

Do you confuse 'which' and 'that'? An easy rule: Choose the one that sounds right. A technical rule: THAT introduces restrictive clauses: I'm looking for the book *that* I heard reviewed on NPR yesterday. WHICH introduces nonrestrictive clauses: The book, *which* had a magnificent cover, was lost forever. *Go back through exercises and make changes.*

DAY **193**

Mother and DAUGHTER

You are a mother, shopping for clothes for the new school year with your teenage daughter. You don't approve of her choices. Start with:

I'm sorry, but it's too ...

TAKE THE NEXT STEP

"Insects sting, not in malice, but because they want to live. It is the same with critics; they desire our blood, not our pain." ~Neitzsche. *Write back to a critic.*

Camp Pain

ONE

Write two words about fighting:
Write two words about camping:
Write two words about friendship:

You are twelve years old and away at overnight camp. You just had a fight with your best friend. Write a letter home, incorporating the words you listed above.

Dear_____,
I'm never talking to_____ever again.
Today ...

> **TAKE THE NEXT STEP**
>
> You can't always change a situation, but you can change who you are in the circumstance. Describe a current challenging situation. Describe who you might be (instead of your usual self) to make it better. Be this person tomorrow and see what happens.

Fun & Games One

Use each word in the left column in the line in which it appears.

Start with: *I remember that game we used to play ...*

war _____

_____

_____

balderdash _____

_____

_____

horse shoes _____

_____

_____

marbles _____

_____

_____

tag _____

_____

_____

spit _____

_____

_____

_____

TAKE THE NEXT STEP

If you met up with your three-year-old, playful self, what one question do you think she or he would ask you about your writing?

What's your answer?

Upside down

Turning things over

doesn't only have to happen in your mind! For this exercise, try a new perspective by turning the book

TAKE THE NEXT STEP

If you don't know what success looks like or feels like, then how will you recognize or enjoy it when it happens? (It may be happening right now!) Write what success feels or looks like for you.

I didn't know ...

upside down. Use the starter provided.

ONE-LINERS

In this story, use as many of these Henny Youngman one-liners as you possibly can (or possibly can stand!):

Answers are what we have for other people's problems.
To a bachelor, marriage means domain poisoning.
A Sunday picnic with the kids is no picnic.
Love is blind, but self-love is full of I's.
Alimony is a case of wife and debt.
To a bald man dandruff is a thrill.
Home is where the mortgage is.
A little gossip goes a long way.
Even his car is shiftless.
He who laughs, lasts.
Take my wife, please.

Start with:
The place was a real dump …

TAKE THE NEXT STEP

If your mental state is overloaded like a dump yard, it's hard to write. List things you need to clear from your mind to make more room for writing.

Your mind is now clear. Start writing!!!

DAY **198**

WET N' WILD

**For an extra challenge, write a story and
DO NOT use any of these words:**

waves pond pool ocean
stream wet swim liquid water
drink flow float creek
deep

Start with:
*Like a fish, I spent
my summer ...*

TAKE THE NEXT STEP

Of all the words above, which one describes your writer-self? Why? Do you want this word to be pertinent a year from now as well? If not, what other word would you like? Why?

Two Coats

Use these words in your story:

Roller   Brush   Paint   Spackle   Coveralls

Start with: *My first coat that wasn't
a hand-me-down …*

TAKE THE NEXT STEP

Do you see (creative) writing as a luxury or a
necessity? Why? How does this point of view
help or hurt your writing practice?

Gender Bender - One

If you are female, write as if you are a retired male New York police officer who lives with ten cats. If you are male, write as if you are a retired female receptionist from New York who lives with twenty cats.

Start with: *I remember that day in July when it hailed ...*

TAKE THE NEXT STEP

What preconceived judgments about yourself get in your way of writing? Tomorrow when you write, choose to be a nonjudgmental blank slate. See what comes.

DAY201

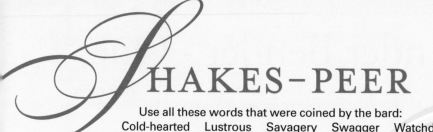

$\mathcal{S}$HAKES‑PEER

Use all these words that were coined by the bard:
Cold-hearted   Lustrous   Savagery   Swagger   Watchdog

Start with: *Even though seeing him makes me shake, I still consider him my peer ...*

TAKE THE NEXT STEP

Role models are not to be feared. Who in your life could be a role model for your writing practice? Think out of the box—it doesn't have to be a writer. Spend more time with him or her. For whom could your writing practice be a role model? Contact him or her and spend time together.

run on

WRITE ONE SENTENCE CONSISTING OF 26 WORDS WHERE EACH WORD BEGINS WITH CONSECUTIVE LETTERS OF THE ALPHABET. START WITH THE LETTER R. (EXAMPLE: ROBERT SAID THAT ULYSSES VIBRATED WILLIAMS' XYLOPHONE YESTERDAY ZEALOUSLY AS BECKY CALLED DAVID'S ELOQUENT FATHER GEORGE HARRISON ISAACSON JOKINGLY KIDDING LOSING MANY NICE OPPORTUNITIES QUICKLY.)

R

S

T

U

V

W

X

Y

Z

A

B

C

D

E

F

G

H

I

J

K

L

M

N

O

P

Q

TAKE THE NEXT STEP

In 26 words or less, write a writing goal. In 26 words or less, how would you feel one year from now if you attained this goal? Why deprive yourself of this feeling? Get started on that goal!

DAY**203**

ON THE ROAD AGAIN

Finish the story. Start with: *Moving …*

TAKE THE NEXT STEP

The energy of others can move us forward. If you bring your writing goals to fruition, who else will benefit? How? *Use their energy to move your writing not only forward, but also up to the next level.*

DAY**204**

DIFFERENT DIRECTIONS

Use the words as you get to them. Start with: The first time I sat on the ...

north

northeast

southeast

south

west

southwest

northwest

east

TAKE THE NEXT STEP

Like life, sometimes our writing takes a very different turn from what we had intended or expected. Write positively about the direction your writing is now headed.

HOT AND BOTHERED · Write eight action words/verbs:

Write eight descriptive words/adjectives:

Use them all in a story. Start with:

It was sweltering hot...

TAKE THE NEXT STEP

On snow days, we take the day off from work and eat, play and accomplish very little. When it's sweltering hot, we often feel like accomplishing little. Today, take a heat day. Get a cool drink, sit back and fan yourself. If, while relaxing, you come up with writing ideas, jot them down.

SPECTRUM

Each time you get to a color on the page, use it in your story.

Start with: The last time ... ------------------------------------

----

--- RED -----------------

------------------------ PURPLE ---------------------------------

----

-- ORANGE ---------------

-------------------------- GREEN --------------------------------

------------------------------- YELLOW --------------------------

----

TAKE THE NEXT STEP

Visualize enjoying your writing success, not
one specific moment, but rather what the full
spectrum of day-to-day enjoyment will look
like and feel like. Visualize it daily so you are
ready when the time comes.

DAY**207**

pick six

Without moving, write down one thing within
your line of vision: an action, person, item, texture, emotion, etc:

. . . .

another thing: . . . .

another thing: . . . .

another thing: . . . .

another thing: . . . .

another thing: . . . .

Now use all six of these
in a piece that begins:
I was frozen in place …

TAKE THE NEXT STEP

My friend Ellen has this quote posted in three places in her office:
"What would you do if you knew you wouldn't fail?" In terms of
your writing, instead of being frozen in inactivity, what would you
do if you knew you wouldn't fail? *Go for it!*

Reminiscing - Two

Imagine talking to a friend from your childhood. Retell and reminisce about favorite times. Use the starting phrases provided.

Do you remember the time we tried …

Do you remember the time we wrote …

Do you remember the time we were asked …

Do you remember the time we quit …

TAKE THE NEXT STEP

If you don't bring your ideas to life by writing them, they will end up being well-kept secrets. When you're writing, imagine you are sharing with a child-hood friend. *Let your pen breathe life into the first sentence of an idea now.*

THE GREAT INQUISITION

Fill in the blanks with the first word that comes to mind:

A landmark:_____   An article of clothing:_____
A cooking verb:_____   A beverage:_____
A planet:_____   A word about glass:_____

Use these six words in your story. Start with: I remember asking ...

TAKE THE NEXT STEP

If you met up with your five-year-old, playful self,
what one question would you like to ask him/her
about creativity? How do you think he/she would
answer?

Truth is Stranger than Fiction

Write an autobiography of a phase of your life. Make sure everything is TRUE except one detail which is 100% made up. Read it to your friends and see if they can pick out the one lie! Start with:

When I was ...

TAKE THE NEXT STEP

Write down two lies you tell yourself about not being good enough.

1.
2.

Now take a thick dark marker and cross out the lies until they are no longer part of your internal repertoire. Feel better?

Flipper 2

In the lines below are five backwards words. When you get to each word, FLIP them in your mind so they become real words. Use that word in your story—before you get to the next word. (Don't read the words first—that spoils the fun!) Start with: I REMEMBER WISHING ...

_____

_____

_____ELCYCIB_____

_____

_____

_____

___NGIS_____

_____

ECAEP_____

_____

_____

_____WOLLIP_____

_____

TAKE THE NEXT STEP

Do you link writing with pain or with pleasure? Why? What can you do to flip your thinking to make it pleasant or more pleasant?

_____

_____EZEEUQS_____

_____

DAY**212**

Stop Write Listen

BEGIN WITH THE STARTING PHRASE PROVIDED. WRITE UNTIL YOU GET TO THE STOP SIGN. EVEN IF YOU ARE IN THE MIDDLE OF A WORD, SENTENCE OR THOUGHT, STOP! BEGIN WRITING WITH THE NEXT STARTING PHRASE. WRITE FROM YOUR HEART. BE HONEST!

START NOW:
WHEN I FACE A BLANK PAGE, I FEEL ...

WHAT I REALLY WANT TO WRITE IS ...

STOP

TAKE THE NEXT STEP

Compose a permission slip, giving yourself permission to write what you want, even if it feels scary. *Next time you sit down to write (or now), start writing what you really want to write.*

August *Augustment*
AUGMENTATION

You are a public school teacher. You love your job, but you really, really, really love your summer vacation. As the warmth of August nears to an end, you wish and pray for it to somehow magically get extended. IT DOES! Write the story. Start with: Sometimes dreams ...

TAKE THE NEXT STEP
List six dreams or realities from the Augusts of your life.

Use these to prompt further writings.

Postcards
without Pictures

You are at the described location, sending a postcard to the specified person. Do all four!

To: A pet

Your location:
Sydney, Australia

To: A family member

Your location:
Anchorage, Alaska

To: A father figure

Your location:
Route 66

To: An ex-spouse

Your location:
Sahara Desert

TAKE THE NEXT STEP

What one thing about your writing practice currently makes you proud?

Write this on a postcard, address it to yourself, and mail it. When it arrives, hang it on the refrigerator like you would a picture postcard sent to you from a dear friend.

DAY 215

Hodge
Podge

Write the name of a neighbor from your childhood:

An expression that a friend overuses:

An odd personality quirk of a relative:

A physical attribute you wish you had:

This is now **YOUR** name, an expression **YOU** overuse and **YOUR** personality quirk. You are also in the middle of dealing with your physical attribute problem! Write in the first person, from the perspective of this new person.

Start with: *Not to burst your bubble …*

TAKE THE NEXT STEP

If you could put your name plus one word describing your writer-self inside a clear bubble that will travel the globe and be seen by millions, what would that one word be? (If you're having trouble, list many and eliminate some daily.)

Peephole - One

You look through the peephole of your front door and see this 👂.
Play out the story. Start with: *I'm a bit of a …*

TAKE THE NEXT STEP

If you could look through a peephole and see that one of your writing projects has been completed, which project would you see and what would it look like? Be specific. Do something today to move this project forward.

Decisions

Use the words on the page as you get to them. Start with: *The Nun didn't …*

_____either_____

_____

_____

or_____

_____

_____

_____if_____then_____

_____

_____

_____

_____instead of_____

_____

_____and_____

_____

_____neither_____

_____

_____

TAKE THE NEXT STEP

What are the top three things you do in order to avoid writing?

1.
2.
3.

Make a decision to NOT do one of them for an entire week and
write instead. Start … now!

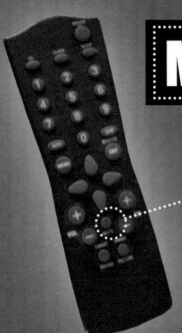

MUTE BUTTON

Use as many of the following in your story as you can:

VOLUME   CHANNEL   59

LAST   02   CONTROL

FAVORITE   UP   SELECT

15   REMOTE   67

RECORD   DOWN

Start with: If the mute button worked on people, I'd …

TAKE THE NEXT STEP

"The most essential gift for a good writer is a built-in shockproof shit-detector." *– Hemingway*

Go back through this exercise and cross out all the B.S. until you're down to the essence of the story. Which of the two versions do you prefer? Why?

BLANK STARE

Finish the story. *For the fourth hour in a row she stared at the blank screen …*

TAKE THE NEXT STEP

If a tree is recognized by its fruit … What is it about your writing style that makes it easily recognizable and unique?

How about your favorite author?

Underdressed &
Under Duress

Free associate with this string of words. Fill this space,
letting one word trigger the next:

Soda, Bubbles, Belch

Now pick three words from your list and use them in a story.
The title of your story is: *Underdressed & Under Duress*

TAKE THE NEXT STEP

When you write in this book is it usually under duress?
What is it that truly motivates you and gets you to
put words on paper? (Dig under the obvious answer.)

Think of this tomorrow when you write.

Waiting in Line

	1	2	3	4	5	6

Start writing down the first column, fill it up, and then write down column two … and so on until you get to the end of the sixth column!

Start with: **Waiting for …**

TAKE THE NEXT STEP
Make believe you're waiting in line at a book signing for your favorite author. What do you tell the people in front of and behind you to get them to buy your writing (now or in the future)? Practice. Whenever you're in line, tell everyone you're a writer.

No, No Barrette

Finish the story. Start with: Back then we all wore our hair ...

TAKE THE NEXT STEP

Often my hair resembles a garden in need of weeding. If your writing practice were a garden, what would you weed out? *What would you plant?*

Bubble Rap 3

Create a dialogue between two people, using the speech bubbles provided.

TAKE THE NEXT STEP

We can rap about what we plan to do until we're blue in the face. Our actions, and in particular, consistency in our actions, is what matters. In what area of your life do you show consistency? How can you transfer this to writing practice?

SURE FOOTING

FINISH THESE SHORTS. STARTERS ARE PROVIDED.

His feet look like Fred Flintstone's ...

They say your feet don't burn when you do a fire walk ...

One slip of the foot and ...

Men with big feet ...

TAKE THE NEXT STEP

Until you put your foot down and actually set a goal—and go for it—you'll never know if you really wanted it in the first place. Nor will you find out what comes up for you that you might want instead. *Create a writing goal. Go for it.*

Hear, Hear 1

Finish the story. Start with:

The first time I heard about him
I had a feeling ...

TAKE THE NEXT STEP

The next time you sit down to write and hear silence instead of your muse, immediately write starting with the phrase, "I don't hear…" Try it now.

Hear, Hear 2

Finish the story.
Start with: From the second I heard about her I knew …

TAKE THE NEXT STEP

Write about the second when you realized that writing was work but you loved it anyway. If this never happened to you, make it up.

DAY**227**

GENDER BENDER

If you are male, write as if you are a female hair-dresser who works from the basement of her home in New Jersey.

If you are female, write as if you are a retired male ranch hand who lives above a drug store in Montana.

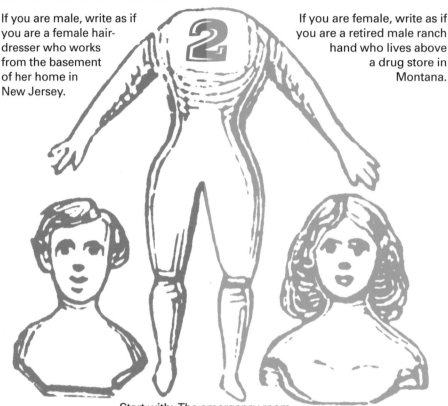

Start with: *The emergency room …*

TAKE THE NEXT STEP

The emergence of a new idea is a wonderful feeling. Describe how it feels to you.

Equate this with something concrete (like a perfect pirouette or riding the largest roller coaster.) Get a picture of this and keep it in your wallet to remind you of your creativity.

CRITIC'S CORNER

ANSWER THE QUESTIONS THAT APPEAR IN THE SHAPES. WRITE (OR DRAW) RIGHT IN THE SHAPES.

WHAT DOES YOUR
INNER CRITIC **SMELL** LIKE?

WHAT DOES YOUR
INNER CRITIC **LOOK** LIKE?

WHAT DOES YOUR
INNER CRITIC **SOUND** LIKE?

WHAT DOES YOUR
INNER CRITIC
FROWN LIKE?

WHAT DOES YOUR
INNER CRITIC **WALK** LIKE?

WHAT ARE SOME OF YOUR
INNER CRITIC'S **FAVORITE WORDS**?

WHAT DO **YOU** SAY OR DO TO
MAKE YOUR INNER CRITIC QUIET
DOWN OR GO AWAY?

TAKE THE NEXT STEP

Where would you like to send your critic? Photocopy this page, put it in an envelope, put proper postage on it, and address it. Then mail it, sending your critic away. Afterward, throw yourself a little party and invite your muse!!

DAY**229**

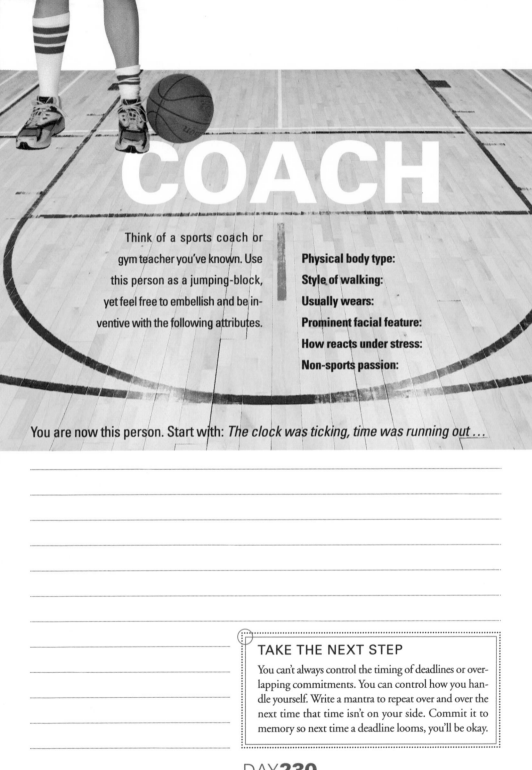

COACH

Think of a sports coach or gym teacher you've known. Use this person as a jumping-block, yet feel free to embellish and be inventive with the following attributes.

Physical body type:

Style of walking:

Usually wears:

Prominent facial feature:

How reacts under stress:

Non-sports passion:

You are now this person. Start with: *The clock was ticking, time was running out …*

TAKE THE NEXT STEP

You can't always control the timing of deadlines or overlapping commitments. You can control how you handle yourself. Write a mantra to repeat over and over the next time that time isn't on your side. Commit it to memory so next time a deadline looms, you'll be okay.

TRUTH OR DARE

Think about a personal truth that very few people know. Now write down the ultimate dare to which you'd be willing to subject yourself in order for this to remain a secret. Write the dare here.

For this story you are now a being in the year 3030, named RoTon. Write from RoTon's point of view making sure to incorporate the aforementioned dare somewhere in the piece. Start with: *The lights went twink and the carrialet began to …*

TAKE THE NEXT STEP

Think of something you have now because you dared to overcome obstacles in the past. It sure looks different in hindsight, doesn't it? Write a lesson you learned to help yourself overcome a current creative obstacle.

SQUEAKY WHEEL

Write down six sounds or noises from kids' toys:

1.
2.
3.
4.
5.
6.

—Squeak, squeak!

—Squeak!

—Squeak, squeak

Use as many of these sounds as you can in a story starting with:

The laser beam penetrated ...

In Tent and In Tents

Finish the story. Start with: *I doubt his intent had been to be so intense …*

TAKE THE NEXT STEP

Next time you pick up this book, let go of the intensity and smile—a big ear-to-ear grin. Keep it on your face while you write. What do you expect will happen to your writing? Tomorrow, check back and see if your prediction was right or wrong.

High Ryes

Finish the story. Start with:

The building where the bread bakery from my childhood used to be ...

TAKE THE NEXT STEP

Money is definitely a motivator. But, other than making some bread, what are other direct and indirect benefits you get from writing? Remind yourself of these often.

TAKE A LETTER - [1]

Whenever you get to one of the letters scattered on the page, use it in a word. It can be the first letter of the word, in the middle, or the last letter of the word. Try basing your story on something autobiographical ... but feel free to embellish to your heart's content. Start with: About the same time every year ...

f

h   r

           x

    y   p

        b   f

  c   n

        u

                          j   t

w

                                    m

                l

e

d

                    j   o

        q

                    z

    a   e

                    j   o

      u   r

        s   g

t

TAKE THE NEXT STEP

Are your computer files, handwritten drafts, and hard copies scattered all over your home or office, like the letters on this page? Or are they all typed, filed, and catalogued? What one thing can you do today to externally show a commitment to your writing? Do it. Then notice how it's reflected in your writing.

DAY235

Double Trouble

All these words have two (or more) meanings.
Use each word at least twice, one for each definition:

bat   press   pen   ring   fly   plug   club   note   band

Start with: The trouble with ...

TAKE THE NEXT STEP

What do the writing monsters that trouble you (who perhaps live under your desk) look like?

Instead of slaying them, what can you do to befriend the monsters and use them to your advantage?

DAY**236**

Danger Us

Finish the story. Start with:
That was, by far, the most dangerous thing I've ever …

TAKE THE NEXT STEP

Sometimes we don't write for fear there will be (dangerous) repercussions from what we put on paper. Nowhere in the definition of writing does it say we must share with others. Write what you want. But first (right now) hug yourself by wrapping your arms around yourself while reminding yourself that you are safe. *Go ahead—do it. It feels good!*

VVhat a character! 3

Pick an age between 48-98: _____

Hair color: _____

Eye color: _____

Name of a city/town: _____

Type of residence/house: _____

Last name starting with R: _____

First name starting with S: _____

Pet peeve: _____

Favorite place to go: _____

You are now officially this character. Write starting with: *The meteor ...*

_____
_____
_____
_____
_____
_____
_____
_____
_____
_____
_____
_____

TAKE THE NEXT STEP

Mobiles that hang over babies' cribs don't usually have meteors on them. But they do have stars, moons, suns, and other things to gently stimulate the baby. What six stimulating things would you put on a mobile to hang over your writing area? *Perhaps you should make one.*

VED-*DY* IN- *TER*-ES- *TINK!*

Think of an accent or dialect you like. Write using that accent. Spell the words the way they sound when pronounced. If you were writing with a German accent, THINK would be written TINK, and WHAT would be VHAT. If it's a Boston accent, PARK would be PAHK, CAR would be CAH.

Start with: *The moment I arrived ...*

DAY**239**

CAMP PAIN - TWO

Write two words about peace: _____
Write two words about elections: _____
Write two words about enemies: _____

You are the best friend of the writer from the exercise titled Camp Pain - One (Day 195). After your fight, you are also writing a letter home. Incorporate the six words from above.

Dear _____,
I don't want to hear the name _____ ever again.
Today ...

TAKE THE NEXT STEP

Many famous people have monikers by which they are known, such as 'Queen of How-To,' 'Polish Prince,' and 'The Refrigerator.' I call myself the 'Muse of Amusement.' Come up with one to describe your writer-self.

Get in the right frame of mind by repeating your moniker aloud as you sit down to write.

MIX-AND-MATCH MUSIC

Write down the following.
Something you buy in a bakery:
A smell from a museum:
An automobile manufacturer:
Something people use to adorn themselves:
An expression that is overused:
A sound from a child's toy:

Use all six items in your writing. Start with:
The music was loud ...

TAKE THE NEXT STEP

End of summer crickets are annoying to some, and like music to others. However, crickets are persistent and stand out from the crowd of other noises. Be your own cricket by always singing (or humming) a theme song to stay on the writing practice path. Write some lyrics for yourself.

PICK SIX - THREE

Without moving, write down one thing within your line of vision:
an action, person, item, texture, emotion, etc:

_____

Another thing: _____

Another thing: _____

Another thing: _____

Another thing: _____

Another thing: _____

Now use all six of these in a piece that begins: *From out of the blue ...*

TAKE THE NEXT STEP

It's tough on your muse to always have to appear from out of the blue. Make it easier by creating a ritual around your writing time and place. Perhaps light a candle at the beginning of the session and extinguish it at the end. Devise a ritual that works for you.

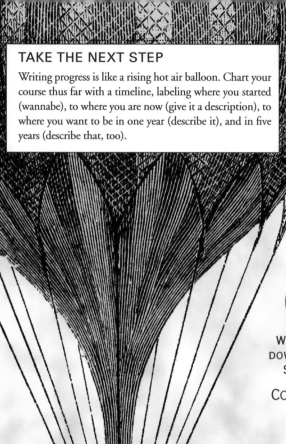

TAKE THE NEXT STEP

Writing progress is like a rising hot air balloon. Chart your course thus far with a timeline, labeling where you started (wannabe), to where you are now (give it a description), to where you want to be in one year (describe it), and in five years (describe that, too).

ONE FROM
COLUMN A

WRITE DOWN COLUMN A FIRST, CONTINUE
DOWN COLUMN B, AND FINISH IN COLUMN C.
START WITH: THE HOT AIR BALLOON ...

COLUMN A   COLUMN B   COLUMN C

DAY**243**

MAKING HEADLINES

You wake up one morning to the following newspaper story about you. Use this title:

Nunc mollis, mauris in tincidunt iaculis, dictum mauris, et iaculis justo felis vehic Praesent leo. Nullam elementum rutrum

WRITER STRIKES IT BIG

TAKE THE NEXT STEP

Practice your autograph so it reflects your writer personality: flowery, large, parochial, sloppy, neat, tight, all caps, etc.

SEPT*ic*

SEPT*uplet*

SEPT*uagenarian*

SEPT*illion*

SEPT*ennial*

SEPT*ilateral*

SEPT*um*

Use these seven words.
Start with: *We took separate …*

SEPTember

TAKE THE NEXT STEP

Separate six memories from the Septembers
of your life and note them here.

Use these to prompt further writings.

DAY**245**

First Grade ★ ★ ★

You are a first grader. Write from this perspective. Be inventive and playful! Give yourself a name with these initials:

N _____ K _____ H _____

A nickname: _____   How you treat them: _____
Eye color: _____   How they treat you: _____
Hair color: _____   Favorite food: _____
Siblings' ages/names: _____ Thoughts on school: _____

Start with: Here I am, the first day of first grade ...

TAKE THE NEXT STEP

In pursuit of goals and life passions, at some point we all fail. It's part of the process. Without these experiences we'd never appreciate our accomplishments, discover our strengths, or know who our real friends are. List one such experience and what you learned from it.

DAY**246**

My Summer Vacation

When telling the stories of your life, there's a lot of freedom in writing about what you haven't done! Use the starting phrase and fill the page.

This past summer I didn't …

TAKE THE NEXT STEP

This past summer I didn't go to a horse race. Did you? If you were a betting person, would you bet more money that you'll keep up your writing practice or that you'll abandon it? Why? If you had to bet in favor of keeping up your practice, how much would you risk?

corner pocket

TAKE THE NEXT STEP

Wander around now in search of an action worth recording (done by another person, an animal, mother nature, etc.) Describe it. If you like, keep a mini notebook in your pocket and record one action daily to fill the book.

Finish this story. Start with: He hustled everyone who came in to Mort's Billiards except ...

Lip Service

Finish these shorts.
Starters are provided.

 She puckered her lips ...

 Watching her apply lipstick ...

 Her pouting lips ...

> ## TAKE THE NEXT STEP
> Make a long list of things that bring a smile to your lips, including three facets of writing.
>
> *Are you smiling now?*

 His lip curled whenever ...

Circle Game - 2

Circle two words that appeal to you:
Peep   Quest   Rotten   Sunshine   Tarantula   Undulate

Circle two words that appeal to you:
Viola   Web   Xylophone   Zipper   Astronaut   Barracuda

Circle two words that appeal to you:
Calliope   Desert   Elegant   Finesse   German   Hysterical

Use these six words in a story. Start with:
I was completely captivated, like a ...

TAKE THE NEXT STEP

"An exclamation mark is like laughing at your own joke." *- F. Scott Fitzgerald.*

Exclamations seem to force the reader to feel something. You've got a captive audience … Don't lose them with exclamation overuse. Show them, don't force them. Go back through this book and eliminate as many exclamations as you can. Now! (oops)

Start with the idiom:

I can't put my finger on it, but ...

Use the idiomatic expression *Head and shoulders above the rest* in your conclusion.

TAKE THE NEXT STEP

Who was head and shoulders above the rest in terms of encouraging your creativity? (Even if they only encouraged you a teeny bit.) Write a two-line thank you to him or her.

Sounds Like ...

B C D G J K L O P R T U X Y

Use all the above letters as initials, letters, or as the words and names they also sound like.
Start with: *We were in alphabetical order ...*

TAKE THE NEXT STEP

Sometimes the alphabet isn't sufficient to make
a point. Many artists sign their paintings with a
symbol. Create one to reflect your writer-self. If
you can draw stick figures, you can do this!!

IF IT AIN'T BROKE

Finish the story. Start with:

It's not like it hasn't been BROKEN before ...

TAKE THE NEXT STEP

What does your creative writing cycle look like? Undulating lines, uphill diagonal, scattered broken lines, etc.? Draw a map to depict it. Add next week's practice, too.

DAY**253**

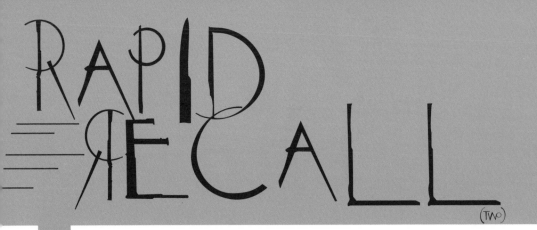

RAPID RECALL

(TWO)

Write the first thing that comes to mind, even if it's not at all true. Use the starters provided. Do all four at once. Don't stop to think. Write fast!

I recall wincing …

That's not at all how I recall what happened …

I remember faces but I never recall the names that go with them. For example …

Recalling the past makes me want to …

TAKE THE NEXT STEP

Whether you have a tendency to look back and recall life or to project forward in life, you can use it to your writing advantage. Look-backers can write memoir, Look-aheaders can write science fiction. Based on this, brainstorm some ideas.

Psychic Totline

Psychic Totline

You're a frustrated, cynical, un-
employed, recent college graduate
with a degree in philosophy. You've been
watching lots of TV. Desperate to find out if
you'll get the university job you applied for,
you call the Psychic Totline, run by a precocious
twelve-year old, reputed to be the reincarnation
of Nostradamus. The kid offers you a job. What if
he really CAN see into the future? Why does he
want to hire you? What do you say?

TAKE THE NEXT STEP

How is your writer-self similar or different from
the self you show the outside world? Explain.

DAY**255**

CR8-A-Character

Write a religious trait/observation you associate with a parent or sibling:

Write about a food a childhood friend ate and the funny way they ate it:

Write something a teacher always wears/wore that's unique to them:

Write a saying someone you know always says:

Create a name using the initials S and P:

You've created a character with these four traits. Write from their point of view. Start with: *I wish I could stop worrying about whether or not …*

TAKE THE NEXT STEP

When you have a long to-do list, do you spend time worrying about the list instead of using the time to write?

Write first. You'll be more motivated to do the list after you do something for yourself.

DAY**256**

FRAMED

Use the shape as you choose.
A starter has been provided.

I was framed ...

TAKE THE NEXT STEP

Do you ever blame someone/something for where you are creatively? Do you ever give someone else credit when you have a creative success? Name the blame/credit source here:_____

Now get a thick marker and cross out the name. You, and only you, are responsible for your creative successes and challenges.

Dial a Dialogue

You are an actress
who makes her living
doing commercials. You are
also the owner of a duplex, a home
with two units, one on top of the other.
You live on the bottom floor, and rent out the
top floor to an undercover policeman. There's a little
tension (actually, a BIG disagreement) between the two
of you. Play it out through a dialogue over the phone:

You: Every time you ...

Cop:

You:

Cop:

You:

Cop:

You:

Cop:

You:

Cop:

You:

Cop:

TAKE THE NEXT STEP

Every time you have an appointment, are you an early bird, right on time, late, no show?

Does your writing practice reflect this other life pattern? What can you do to have balance in both?

... and since you're the writer, YOU get the last word!

You:

DAY**258**

Naming Names – *Two*

Finish all four of these shorts. The starter will stay constant but your name will change.

Your name is Ashley. Start with: The plaid shirt ...

Your name is Fanny. Start with: The plaid shirt ...

Your name is Tab. Start with: The plaid shirt ...

Your name is Maurice. Start with: The plaid shirt ...

TAKE THE NEXT STEP

If you were to name your writer-self and the first three letters of each name had to be PRO, would you be PROfessor PROcrastinator PROmetheus? PROlific PROcess PROfit? Or another? Be a PROfessional writer and give yourself a first, middle, and last name all beginning with PRO.

Disaster Averted

Use these four words: TICKLE   TEAR   RITE   LOCKET

Start with: *What a disaster ...*

TAKE THE NEXT STEP

No need for tomorrow's writing practice to even have a chance at disaster. Write the ideal writing horoscope for yourself. Read it to-morrow before you write to make sure all its predictions come true.

fresh air

fresh

Start with the word _air_ and write a story or poem, using each letter as you get to it!

AIR
B
C
d
E
f
g
H
i
j
K
L
M
N
O
Q
R
s
T
u
V
W
X
Z

TAKE THE NEXT STEP

Fresh Air is a great NPR program. Start to prep now for your interview by answering these questions aloud in front of a mirror.

1. If you had to do it all over, what would you do the same?
2. What's the story behind how you got started?
3. Who has been your biggest influence, and why?
4. What's a piece of advice you can offer others starting out?

NOT GUILTY

**FINISH THE STORY.
START WITH: IT WAS A
TIME OF INNOCENCE …**

TAKE THE NEXT STEP

I confess. I don't exercise. Whenever I walk past my exercise equipment, I feel guilty. What can you do in your writing practice to not experience any guilt at all?

TAKE A LETTER
(2)

Whenever you get to one of the letters scattered on the page, use it in a word.
It can be the first letter of the word, in the middle, or the last letter of the word.
Try basing your story on something autobiographical … but feel free
to embellish to your heart's content. Start with: *The dog days were …*

_____ A_____
_____ B_____
_____ C_____
_____ D_____
_G_____ E_____
_____ F_____
_H_____ I_____
_J_____ K_____
_____ N_____ M_____
_____ L
_____ O_____
_P_____
_____ R_____
_Q_____
_____ S_____
_____ T_____
_____ U_____
_____ V_____
_____ W_____
_X_____ Y_____
_____ Z_____ B_____
_____ G_____ N_____ O__
_I_____ L_____

TAKE THE NEXT STEP

Writing can often be like walking an independent-minded dog. It wants to go in one direction when you want to go in another. One way to handle this is to put an editing mark in the margin, briefly note the direction you want to go, and then see where the writing leads. Invent your own unique editing mark.

ANTICIPATION

Write a story about something that is just about to happen.
Start with: *I was about to burst …*

DAY**264**

fun & games 2

Use each word in the left column in the
line in which it appears. Start with:
Sometimes the most fun can be had …

_____
_____
_____
_____

monopoly_____
_____
_____

perfection_____
_____
_____

twister_____
_____
_____

outburst_____
_____
_____

cranium_____
_____
_____

risk_____
_____
_____

TAKE THE NEXT STEP

Gift giving and receiving both feel wonderful. Here's a chance to double your fun. What's the best inexpensive (or free) gift you can give your writer-self? *Write steps on how you'll go about giving this gift to yourself.*

DAY**265**

Finish the story.
Start with: *She whispered* ...

Soft Spoken

TAKE THE NEXT STEP

To keep up with writing practice, you need to
say (not whisper) NO to others. Jot down ways
to say no to invitations because you already
have a date with yourself to write. This will
help you to say NO out loud.

DAY**266**

FACTIONS OF FRACTIONS

Use the fractions as you get to them. Start with: If it appears as if I am thinking with a fraction of my brain ...

$\frac{1}{2}$

$\frac{1}{4}$

$\frac{1}{8}$

$\frac{2}{3}$

$\frac{3}{4}$

$\frac{3}{8}$

TAKE THE NEXT STEP

Fill each of the sixteen boxes in the grid with a word taken from the writing you already did on this page. You'll end up with a poem that reads from left to right, top to bottom.

The Green Room

Use the starting phrase and fill the page.

I was in one of my mint green moods the day ...

TAKE THE NEXT STEP

Whether you're in the green room or food shopping, as long as there are smells, you can always practice writing. Write the first thing that comes to mind based on each of these smells.

Spearmint:

Paint remover:

Strong perfume:

Hate to Love

With a series of one-letter changes, the word hate turns to love.

HATE   RATE   RAVE   CAVE   COVE   LOVE

Use all six of these words in this piece.

Start with: *The Eskimos …*

TAKE THE NEXT STEP

Your writing is thrilled that you are giving it so much time and attention. It's so thrilled, it is now writing you a love note. Lend it your pen and hand so the message is legible.

Basement

Picture a basement/cellar from your childhood. Mentally open the door, descend the stairs, feel the banister, take in the smells, notice the quality of light, what's on the steps, floor, walls. Hear the sound of the pipes, and the other noises. Behind a hot water heater, in the shadows, is something you never noticed before... an old wooden door! You go to it, take the knob in your hand, turn it ... Now start writing!

TAKE THE NEXT STEP

If you were to host a writing party, would a basement be a good setting? What location, games, snacks, events, entertainment would you provide? *Invite others or throw yourself a party for two— you and your muse!*

Moral - One

Use the moral at the bottom of the page to conclude the story you are about to write. Start with: *Back when I was …*

And the moral of the story is:
The apple doesn't fall far from the tree.

TAKE THE NEXT STEP

I promised myself that when I got a book deal I'd buy myself a fruit-of-the-month club. Whenever a catalog arrived I was reminded of my prize and my progress. What gift would you choose? What goal do you want to attain? Call now to make sure you receive the catalog regularly.

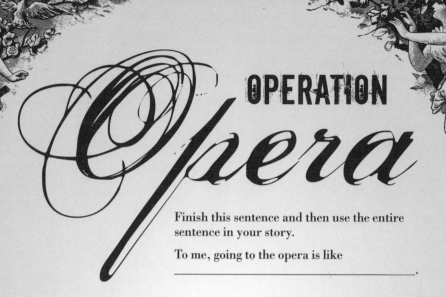

OPERATION

Opera

Finish this sentence and then use the entire sentence in your story.

To me, going to the opera is like

_____.

Start with: *The covert operation was ...*

_____

_____

_____

_____

_____

_____

_____

TAKE THE NEXT STEP

If your muse were to take you out on a date, where do you think he or she would take you? Opera? Monster truck rally? Fishing? Why?

DAY**272**

what a coincidence

Life is full of coincidences. Write about one that actually happened to you.
Start with: *What a coincidence …*

TAKE THE NEXT STEP

It's not a coincidence that ideas come when we're
shopping. Describe this character based solely on cart
contents: orange flip flops, a deadbolt lock replacement
kit, and a twelve-pack of yellow legal pads.

Try this the next time you shop.

Tag-Two

In Pennsylvania most license plates are three letters and four numbers. Example: CAD 2322. For this exercise, use the three letters as the first letters of the three beginning words in your story. Example: Come And Donate. Use the four digit number, 2322, somewhere in your story. Example: Make your donations at Smiley Bank at 2322 Main Street. Start here ...

TAKE THE NEXT STEP

Playing tag was a carefree way to spend summer evenings. If there were no deadlines and no expectations, what would be your writing equivalent to playing tag?

Look ... You've already started to play.

Two Life Sentences

Use these two sentences about life in your story:

1. Life is like drawing without an eraser. (Anon)
2. Life shrinks or expands in proportion to one's courage. (Anaïs Nin)

Start with: *The bloody* ...

TAKE THE NEXT STEP

When it comes to life, are you a mental pre-planner? A spontaneous jump-right-in-er? A plodder? A present-is-a-gift-er? A procrastinator? A lamenter of missed chances?

How is this reflected in your writing practice?

Spin The Bottle

finish the story. Start with:
At my first boy-girl party I ...

TAKE THE NEXT STEP

A fun writing exercise is to give titles to your
current life as if it was a ...

Teen movie:
Romance novel:
Sitcom:
Country song:
Mystery novel:
Home and garden show:

Handy

Finish these shorts. Starters are provided.

Her hands were so delicate …

He took my hand in his …

The calluses on his hands …

I have to hand it to you …

TAKE THE NEXT STEP

Close your eyes and explore your hands with your hands as if for the first time. They deliver the writing goods, yet we barely know them. When done, write one thing that surprised you about what came to mind.

DAY**277**

Setting Sun

Set this story during an eclipse. Start with: The light was ...

TAKE THE NEXT STEP

List six enlightening memories from your Octobers of yore.
Use these to prompt further writings.

DAY**278**

Onomatopoeia

Onomatopoetic words imitate sounds associated with the objects or actions they refer to. Here is a long list. Feel free to add more of your own!

Hiss, ping, crunch, pop, sizzle, bang, swish, smash, flutter, clunk, peck, whistle, smack, whack, hush, whir, tiptoe, whoosh, thud, zap, twang, cock-a-doodle-doo, squish, stomp, tap, thump, splash, purr, tinkle, gush, ker-plunk, slurp, swirl, crash, whirl, clang, mumble, squeak, boom, meow, plop, cuckoo, pow, splat, quack, screech, zoom, tick tock, burp, clip clop, eek, hiccup, moo, oink, buzz

Now, using the first line of Edgar Allen Poe's "The Tell-Tale Heart," write your own story incorporating as many of these words as possible.

"True! Nervous, very, very dreadfully nervous I had been and I am: but why will you say that I am mad?"

TAKE THE NEXT STEP

Another example of a writing practice that can be done anywhere is to simply listen to what's going on. Write the first thing that comes to mind from these sounds.

Ticking:
Grinding teeth:
Popped balloon:
Rain on metal:

WHAT IF ?

Finish the story.
What if, at will, people could grow more than two arms?

Try to channel excess energies
into rejuvenation.
Lucky Numbers 11, 16, 30, 43, 45, 48

TAKE THE NEXT STEP

If you could put a dollar value on your current writing assets plus your untapped writing potential, how much would they be worth? What can you do to protect this investment? What can you do to grow this investment?

TAKE A LETTER - THREE

Whenever you get to one of the letters scattered on the page, use it in a word. It can be the first letter of the word, in the middle, or the last letter of the word. Try basing your story on something autobiographical … but feel free to embellish to your heart's content. Start with: *Mysteries make me …*

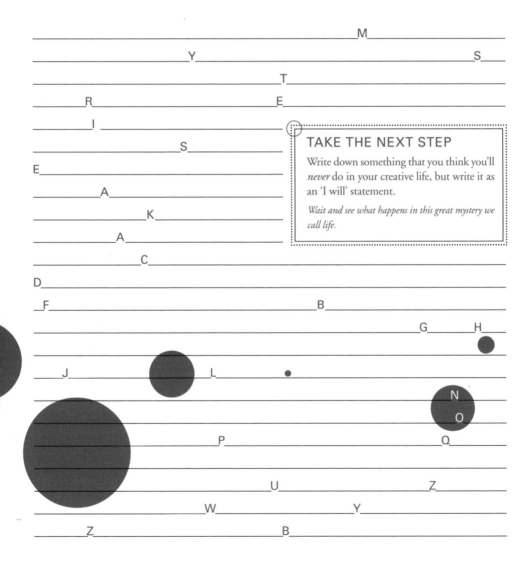

_____ M_____

_____ Y_____ S____

_____ T_____

_____ R_____ E_____

_____ I _____

_____ S_____

E_____

_____ A_____

_____ K_____

_____ A_____

_____ C_____

D_____

_F_____ B_____

_____ G_____ H_____

__ J_____ L_____ •_____

_____ N

_____ O

_____ P_____ Q_____

_____ U_____ Z_____

_____ W_____ Y_____

__ Z_____ B_____

> **TAKE THE NEXT STEP**
>
> Write down something that you think you'll *never* do in your creative life, but write it as an 'I will' statement.
>
> *Wait and see what happens in this great mystery we call life.*

Phone Home

This info was taken from a suburban Philadelphia phone book.
Use your own local phone book to repeat the exercise!

Two first names: SANDRA, ARNOLD
Two last names: CHUDNOFF, KRAMER
One restaurant name: LAMB TAVERN
One beauty salon name: WAVELENGTH
One street name: HAMPSHIRE DRIVE

Now write, incorporating as many of the above items as possible.
Start with: *The number was …*

TAKE THE NEXT STEP

Does the phone ring if there's no one to hear it? Have you written
something if you don't ever read it? Go back and read through some
of the exercises you've done. Get a red pen and circle the words/para-
graphs that stand out. Pick up the phone and call your answering
machine and read some of these to yourself. Make them come alive.

ALL MY LIFE'S
A CIRCLE
-TWO-

Circle two words that appeal to you:

MUSHROOM   GEMOLOGIST   MOODY

BUNGALOW   DEBUTANTE   TAXI

Circle two words that appeal to you:

CARNIVORE

DILL   MINIATURE

HARRY   TELEPHONE

TEMPERATURE

Circle two words that appeal to you:

RUBBER   SQUEEZE

POTION   ASPIRIN

CHALKY   BANANAS

Use these six words in a story.
Start with:
It was just after dark …

TAKE THE NEXT STEP

Turn out all the lights and finish this statement while writing in total darkness. *I don't see why …*

DAY**283**

Target Practice

When you write, try to hit your target audience!
Use the starter provided.

My aim is usually better ...

TAKE THE NEXT STEP

Make a list of things you aim to write about in the future. Put each
on a slip of paper (like a fortune cookie) and put them in a jar. Use
them if you're ever wandering aimlessly in the land of writing.

PENCIL ME IN

**Come up with five creative uses for a pencil
(other than a writing implement):**

1.
2.
3.
4.
5.

**Incorporate these five "uses" in this piece.
Start with:** *Whenever I am asked to ...*

TAKE THE NEXT STEP

Write a thank you note to your pen/pencil/keyboard.
Butter him/her up. Don't feel silly. It is your partner.
Where would Fred be without Ginger ... or Wilma?

Early Bird

Finish the story. *I was awakened at the crack of dawn ...*

TAKE THE NEXT STEP

Writing is like fishing. At the crack of dawn you go to a spot you believe is best, put bait on your line, and cast it. The flow, meditation,
and predictability of the steps often lead to surprises. What is your
writing bait? What surprises you about writing?

It Was a Dark and Stormy Night

The #2 most famous opener! Finish this story by using it as the last seven words. Start with the #1 most famous opener.

Once upon a time ...

... it was a dark and stormy night.

TAKE THE NEXT STEP

Animals respond to danger by fight or flight. Same is true for writers. When things get challenging, do you fight by working harder? Or do you run away and abandon your writing? Write about when you stayed and worked something through to success.

snapshots - three

Photos are a great way to capture memories. But we don't always have a camera with us. Write quick "word snapshots" as substitutes for the following topics. Try to capture colors, textures, and expressions. Use your own life story ... or make them up!

An embarrassing moment ...

A religious celebration ...

By a pool ...

In the snow ...

TAKE THE NEXT STEP

Capture a snapshot of the future by closing your eyes and picturing what you want. Do it now and envision success from writing: People listening to you read poetry, someone discovering your journal in 100 years, an audience laughing at your romantic comedy, an article in a magazine or newspaper, sharing your writing to help someone heal, etc.

Fall Leaves Me Wishing

Finish the story. *Every year in mid-October, we take a ride to the Pocono Mountains where we soak up the fall color and visit my husband's colorful relatives. The trip always leaves me wishing …*

TAKE THE NEXT STEP

Many creative people are colorful characters who have limiting beliefs. Like believing you can only write if you have a fine tip black felt pen. Do you have limiting beliefs? Sometimes they are subtle. List a way you can break through obstacles you put in your own way.

VAN GO

Use the following two items in a story: Van Gogh and Van Go. Set it in the year 2121. And start with: The swirl of colors ...

Quota of Quotes

Use as many of the following Ben Franklin quotes in your story as you can:

A penny saved is a penny earned.
Eat to live, and not live to eat.
An empty bag cannot stand upright.
Lost time is never found again.

A stitch in time saves nine.
Some are weatherwise, some are otherwise.
The used key is always bright.
The cat in gloves catches no mice.

Start with: *Not to sound like my ...*

FAMOUS FIRSTS - THREE

Finish the story. Start with: *One day back there in the good old days when I was nine and the world was full of every imaginable kind of magnificence, and life was still a delightful and mysterious dream, my cousin Mourad, who was considered crazy by everybody who knew him except me, came to my house at four in the morning and woke me up by tapping on the window of my room.*

TAKE THE NEXT STEP

What excites you about beginning a project? What scares you about beginning a project? List ideas on how you can turn this fear into excitement every time.

(This first line is from *My Name Is Aram* by William Saroyan.)

Shadow Figures

Use the words as you get to them. Start with: *Shadows don't usually scare me ...*

_____

_____

_____marshmallow_____

_____

mango_____

_____

_____

_____milk_____

_____

_____

_____

_____mud_____

_____

_____

_____mothballs_____

_____

_____

_____mink_____

_____

TAKE THE NEXT STEP

If writing is putting words on paper one after another the way walking is putting one foot in front of the other ... Then what are the shadows that make writing scarier?

DAY**293**

TRISKAIDEKAPHOBIA

Use these thirteen words in your story:

BOOK   AUTHOR   MYSTERY   MONEY   SUCCESS

ROMANCE   WEALTH   MANSION   PLAY

SCIENCE FICTION   STAR   COMMITMENT   BEST SELLER

Start with: I am terribly afraid …

TAKE THE NEXT STEP

There are probably 13 million excuses not to do writing practice. When did you learn to make excuses for something you really want to do? Why do you still do it?

NOCTURNAL

Finish the story. Start with: *He haunted the night like a …*

_____

_____

_____

_____

_____

_____

_____

_____

_____

_____

_____

TAKE THE NEXT STEP

Haunted houses make great settings for stories.
List locations with which you are familiar that
would be good for stories, books, articles, etc.
Pick one and get started now.

Baker's Dozen

- Sweet potato
- That's how the cookie crumbles
- Whipped cream
- Persimmon
- Red as a beet
- Lima beans
- Shrimp cocktail
- Steak
- Passion fruit
- Chocolate
- Cool as a cucumber
- Chicken
- Ice cubes

Use these thirteen "foods" in your story.
Start with: *She dipped …*

....
....
....
....
....
....
....
....
....
....
....
....
....
....
....
....
....
....
....
....
....
....
....
....
....

TAKE THE NEXT STEP

There are lots of ways to feed your writer-self. I like to read. And, breaking a writing rule, I am okay reading a similar genre to what I am in the process of writing. What writing rules have you broken? What writing rules do you abide by?

P.T. BURN 'EM

Use all five of these words in this piece:

PAT   POT   PIT

PET   PUT

Start with:
There certainly is a sucker burned every minute.
Take for example, my . . .

TAKE THE NEXT STEP

When it comes to infomercials, I am a sucker. I want to buy everything. When the announcer says, "Wait, there's more," I get excited. Similar to performers doing an encore, what can you do to add extra oomph for your readers?

PEEPHOLE-2

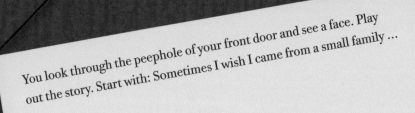

You look through the peephole of your front door and see a face. Play out the story. Start with: Sometimes I wish I came from a small family ...

TAKE THE NEXT STEP

We can't choose our family, but we can choose our friends. Trace your connections until you link yourself to a famous writer. (Like Six Degrees of Kevin Bacon).

Beeeeeee-uuuuuu-teeeeeee-ful

Finish the story.

Start with: *He took one look and whistled a long and drawn out "Beeeee-uuuuu-teeeee-ful ...*

TAKE THE NEXT STEP

From *The Book of Qualities* by J. Ruth Gendler: "Beauty is startling. She wears a gold shawl in the summer and sells seven kinds of honey at the flea market. She is young and old at once ..." Personify your writing practice.

Moral - Two

Use the moral at the bottom of the page to conclude the story you are about to write.
Start with: *The turtle-slow truck ...*

And the moral is: *One man's ceiling is another man's floor.*

TAKE THE NEXT STEP

Imagine the writer part of your personality floating up to the ceiling and looking down at the rest of you. What would he or she tell you to help you be a better writer?

TWENTY *questions—2*

Answer the 20 questions by circling one option. When done, you'll have a character sketch.

Human or Alien?   Big or Little?   Hairy or No hair?   Young or Old?

Mad or Cheery?   Clairvoyant or Oblivious?   Thick-skinned or Thin-skinned?   Honest or Dishonest?   Athletic or Rotund?   Famous or Infamous?

Dog-owner or Cat-owner?   Bold or Wimpy?   Green-thumb or Brown-thumb?

Travels by Boat or Plane?   Vanilla cake or Chocolate cake?   Nail Biter or Well-manicured?
Reader or Writer?   Technophile or Technophobe?

Boxers or Briefs?   Paper or Plastic?

You are this person.

Write from their perspective. Start with:

I couldn't stop …

TAKE THE NEXT STEP

If your writer-self were a traffic sign, would you be Stop? Yield? Soft shoulder? How often do you break your own traffic rules? Do you need to choose another sign? Which one? Why?

walk *the* LINE

Write only on the lines as provided. Start with:
What started out as a casual walk …

_____
_____
_____
_____
_____
_____
_____
_____
_____
_____
_____
_____
_____
_____
_____
_____
_____
_____
_____
_____

TAKE THE NEXT STEP

Think of the very last person you saw or spoke to. If you were to 'walk in their shoes,' what would the new you write about? Can you turn one of these ideas into a project?

Fall Back

Finish the story. Start with: *Sometimes it's best not to have a safety net to fall back on . . .*

TAKE THE NEXT STEP

Trace back through your entire life, listing all the stepping stone episodes that led to this writing exercise in this book today. Pretty cool, huh?

Haunted Castle

You've been invited to spend a night at a haunted castle. List the top six things you'd pack:

1.
2.
3.
4.
5.
6.

Use them all in a story. Start with: *Sometimes glamour …*

TAKE THE NEXT STEP

If you had to pack up quickly and leave your home, would you grab any of your writing? If so, which items? If not, what do you need to do to get your writing on this priority list?

MONSTER MASH

Use the words as you get to them.
Start with:

Monsters don't ...

MASH

BASH

DASH

GASH

LASH

RASH

TAKE THE NEXT STEP

"Don't think and then write it down. Think on paper."

~ Harry Kemelman

Here's a chance to not reHASH. *Write exactly what comes to mind at this moment.*

NovemBERTH

Finish the story. Start with: *I found myself in the berth of the spaceship November …*

TAKE THE NEXT STEP

Travel back mentally and list six memories from Novembers past.

Use these to prompt further writings.

PECULIAR PET

Pick one of these peculiar pets:

**HOARSE GIRAFFE   HUMMINGBIRD AFRAID OF HEIGHTS
COCKROACH AFRAID OF THE DARK   NEUROTIC APE
CAT ALLERGIC TO CATS   3-LEGGED GOAT   20-POUND MOUSE
TIGER WITH AN INGROWN TOENAIL**

You are now this pet. Write using its voice and point of view. Tell us your name, where you came from, what you do all day, and how your new owner has reacted to owning you. Start with: *The folks at the ...*

TAKE THE NEXT STEP

Write an ad advertising why you as a writer would make the best candidate to adopt a 400-pound turtle. Really make yourself sound good.

Defective Detective

What is the oddest thing someone would find in one of the drawers in your home or office? What's the item? Which drawer? You are a detective investigating a case and you come across this item. Of course it belongs to someone you've never met and is in a place you've never been before. What would you conclude about this unknown person and his/her life? Start with: Hidden under ...

TAKE THE NEXT STEP

Everyone's an expert at something, whether it's being a detective or picking the ripest cantaloupe. List some of your more unusual areas of expertise. Can you turn one or more into writing projects?

DAY**308**

an earful

Finish these shorts. Starters are provided.

He had the biggest ears ...

She always kept her ear to the ground ...

When the pencil got stuck in my ear ...

He could make his ears twitch and his ...

TAKE THE NEXT STEP

Here's a challenge for you. Write a paragraph without using the letters E, A, or R. Start with: *With two ...*

DAY309

Rhyme Time

Write two nouns that rhyme:
Two verbs that rhyme:
Two adjectives that rhyme:
Two names that rhyme:

Write a story using all eight words starting with: *When I asked …*

TAKE THE NEXT STEP

If a genie appeared, what three writing wishes would you make? The criteria for listing them is that they must all rhyme somehow.

Do something now toward making one of them come true.

FICTIONARY ~ THREE

Write a dictionary-style definition for the word *indaba* {pronounced in-DAH-ba}.
Use *indaba* with your fictitious definition in a story. START WITH: The scream was loud …

TAKE THE NEXT STEP

If you were to arrange a conference of mentors, whom would you invite? What's one question you would ask them all?

Answer it yourself.

(The definition of indaba - n. a conference of indigenous peoples of Southern Africa.)

You've Got Malefactors

Finish the story. Start with: *The pickpocket gingerly …*

TAKE THE NEXT STEP

From among all the possibilities, pick out what you'd like
to accomplish in your writing tomorrow. First thing in
the morning, refer to the list and immediately do one of
the things. You'll feel great all day.

DAY312

BIG
CHEESE

Write in and around the pictures
on the page as you choose.

Start with:
He was the most pompous …

TAKE THE NEXT STEP

The more cheese ages, the better
it is. The younger a vegetable is,
the better it tastes. What about
your current age enables you to
be a better writer?

Green With ENVY

Describe your favorite green thing in great detail:

Now circle five of the most intriguing words from this description and use them in a story. Start with: The leprechaun brought me ...

TAKE THE NEXT STEP

In presentation, color makes an impact. Experiment. Get a pencil and blacken in an area. Now write with the eraser.

DAY**314**

DOUBLE AGENT

Write using the starter. Whatever word it is that you write when you first come to the brackets, you must then use every time you come to a bracket on the rest of the page! Start with: *He's my husband, but he's also a double agent …*

{   }

{   }

{   }

{   }

{   }

{   }

TAKE THE NEXT STEP

Double your productivity by making your goals quantifiable. 'Write every day' is easier to achieve when it is worded 'Write ten minutes a day, three days a week for three months.'

Record two quantifiable writing goals to accomplish in the next two days.

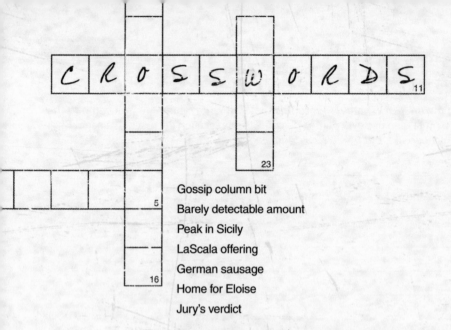

C R O S S W O R D S 11

23

5

16

Gossip column bit

Barely detectable amount

Peak in Sicily

LaScala offering

German sausage

Home for Eloise

Jury's verdict

These are all clues from crossword puzzles. Use them (or the actual answers to the clues) in a story. Start with:

I rarely get cross, but ...

○ TAKE THE NEXT STEP

If you've ever gotten cross with a review, try it yourself. Review a recent book, film, song, or article.

DAY**316**

Wanna Write

On this page, write all the topics you'd like to write about today (or someday.) Separate each topic with a comma and fill all the lines on the page. Be as outrageous as you like. Go over the edge! Approach this with the attitude that the sky's the limit!

TAKE THE NEXT STEP

Did you ever wanna be someone else? If you could be any writer dead or alive, who would you choose and why? What one trait from this person can you add to your writing practice now?

HE-MAIL

Finish the story. Start with: *I met him in an online chat room for people who ...*

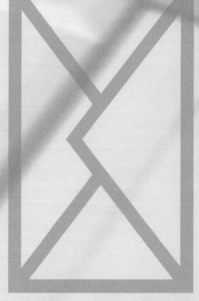

TAKE THE NEXT STEP

The more people you meet and ask for help to accomplish your goals, the more likely you'll succeed. Make a list of people who can help you, or who might know someone who can help. Ask one for assistance today.

Weird Words - Three

Use the words EDDA, IDUN, ATLI, and EGIL in your story—even though you probably don't know what they mean. Set your story during the gold rush. Start with: *The rope was tight . . .*

P.S. All are Norse words. EDDA=prose, IDUN=mythological woman, ATLI=mythological king, EGIL=mythological hero

TAKE THE NEXT STEP

Ever notice how you learn a new word and suddenly it's everywhere? Same thing holds true for thoughts. Focus on something positive you want in your writing life. Write it down. Now see how it appears and what happens.

BALD
BALLERINA

Start with the word BALD and free associate. Write down whatever comes to mind.

BALD: _____

_____

_____

_____

Circle six interesting words (from above). Use them in a story whose main character is a ballerina.

Start with: *I was backstage …* _____

_____

_____

_____

_____

_____

_____

_____

_____

_____

_____

_____

TAKE THE NEXT STEP

Think of a project you've put on the back burner. List the pros and cons to completing it. Whether you choose to finish it or let it go, you'll feel better knowing you made a choice.

I, I, SIR

Whenever you get to the letter I, use it. Start with:

The aisle was ... _____

_____I_____I_____

_____

_____I_____

____I_____I_____I_____

_____I_____

_____

_____I_____

____I_____I_____I_____

_____

_____I_____I_____

_____I_____

_____I_____I_____

_____I_____

____I_____I_____I_____

__I_____

_____I_____I_

_____I_____I_____

_____I_____

_____I_____

_____.

TAKE THE NEXT STEP

Write about yourself. Instead of using first person (I), use second person (you).

Reunion

These twins appeared in a dream you had two nights ago about a fifty-year high school reunion. This was odd because it's only been five years since you left high school. This evening at the supermarket, oddly enough, you ran into one of them and he addressed you by name. Finish the story. Start with: *"Hello William. Did you enjoy …*

TAKE THE NEXT STEP

What about writing do you enjoy? What about writing gives you satisfaction?

DAY322

BEST SEAT IN THE HOUSE

USE THE PICTURES AS YOU LIKE. START WITH:

Leaving the seat up …

TAKE THE NEXT STEP

Get a big bowl, fill it with warm water, and soak your feet while writing. Start with: *I am floating …*

DAY**323**

Song & Dance

Finish the following two sentences:

My singing voice sounds like ...

When I dance I look like ...

Now use these two full sentences in a story that starts with: *We made a left onto Canal Street ...*

TAKE THE NEXT STEP

Compare writing to singing or dancing. How is writing different? How is writing easier? How is writing harder? How are they similar? How can you combine them?

Petite Paragraphs

Here is a chance to write short paragraphs of memory snippets. Use the starters provided.

I remember rushing …

I remember pulling …

I remember pushing …

I remember covering …

I remember deciding …

I remember choosing …

TAKE THE NEXT STEP

Remember what it feels like to be relaxed? Tense every muscle in your body at once and hold for 20-25 seconds. Release and shake it all out. Aaah. Now write.

GIRL TALK

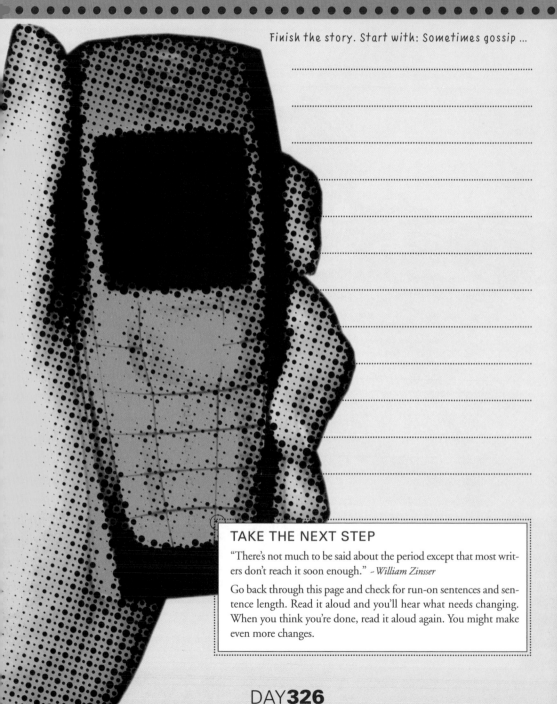

Finish the story. Start with: Sometimes gossip ...

TAKE THE NEXT STEP

"There's not much to be said about the period except that most writers don't reach it soon enough." – *William Zinsser*

Go back through this page and check for run-on sentences and sentence length. Read it aloud and you'll hear what needs changing. When you think you're done, read it aloud again. You might make even more changes.

Greek Gods

Use the Greek gods as you get to them on the page. Start with: *Winning is not …*

_____Ares_____

_____

_____Zeus_____

_____

_____

_____

_____Poseidon_____

_____

_____

_____

_____

_____Apollo_____

_____

_____Eros_____

_____

TAKE THE NEXT STEP

How are you at receiving praise? Do you blush? Smile? Hide?
Look away? Deny it? It feels great to be able to take in every
word. To practice, stare at yourself in a mirror. Make good
eye contact, breathe slowly, touch your heart with one hand,
and praise yourself. Do it until you feel comfortable hearing
wonderful things about yourself.

MELLOW YELLOW

LOOK AROUND YOU AND NOTICE ALL THE
YELLOW THINGS. WRITE DOWN THE FIRST
SIX YOU SEE:

1. _____

2. _____

3. _____

4. _____

5. _____

6. _____

TAKE THE NEXT STEP

Get some wrapping paper (or newspaper, or tape together pieces of copy paper) and wrap this book. Tomorrow when you reach for it you'll be reminded just how much you treasure the gift of writing. Do this with other projects, too. It puts the way you approach and appreciate them in a whole new light. Start wrapping.

USE ALL SIX. START WITH:
ONE MAN'S TREASURE IS ANOTHER MAN'S ...

MORAL-3

Use the moral at the bottom of the page to conclude the story you are about to write. Start with: She watched the sky ...

_____

_____

_____

_____

_____

_____

And the moral of the story: The bigger they come, the harder they fall.

TAKE THE NEXT STEP

Could you pick your inner critic out of a line-up? What would you convict him/her of? What sentence (allow the pun to influence your answer) does he or she deserve? Is it true that 'the bigger they come, the harder they fall'?

Thanks, But No Tanks

List three things from the past 365 days for which you are thankful.

1.

2.

3.

Use all three in a story where you are a container delivery person. Start with:
The aquarium workers were on strike and I couldn't just leave the tank of sharks in the parking lot, so I . . .

TAKE THE NEXT STEP

Think about your writer-self over the last 24 hours. Did you accomplish anything? What, or why not? Were you the best writer you could be? Why or why not? Did you thank your writer-self? How? Let these guide the next 24 hours.

Turkey Day

Finish the story.

What a turkey Uncle Ted was that day . . .

TAKE THE NEXT STEP

If this was an episode of Survivor, for what writing dream to come true would you eat a two-inch cockroach? Is there a writing dream for which you'd you eat six two-inch cockroaches to have it come true?

Objects Not Of *Desire*

Use all these household objects in this story:

Carrot Peeler   Toaster   Floor Lamp   Toilet Bowl Brush   Dish Drainer

Start with: *The long ...*

TAKE THE NEXT STEP

What's the next step in your creative process? Are you resisting it? Don't you desire the end result enough? Or is it something else? What's the worst thing that will happen if you do it? Are you willing to take that risk?

SIGNS OF THE TIMES

Use the traffic sign words as you come to them. Start with: Every time I …

_____

_____

_____SOFT SHOULDER_____

_____

_____

_____

_____

_____

_____YIELD_____

_____

_____

_____

_____

_____MERGE_____

_____

_____

_____

_____

_____

_____SLOW_____

_____

_____.

TAKE THE NEXT STEP

Do you have an idea how much time you spend writing every day? Keep a 24-hour log to see. Include signing checks, making lists, etc. Before you do it, guess how much time you think it amounts to. When done, come back and see how close you were.

STOP

SLAP STICK

You are a world-class body builder. You live in a town called Fishfoot. You just had a fight with your brother, named Slap, who is an air taxi driver. The year is 2525. Your name is Stick. Start your story with: *Slap never understood my love of ...*

TAKE THE NEXT STEP

Here's an exercise to stretch your mental muscle. Describe how the word SLAP pertains to your writing. Now describe how the word STICK does not pertain to your writing. Did you feel the mental burn as you stretched?

Rebus Rebuttal

Instead of words, this exercise has pictures. Use them as you come to them.
Start with: *After the debate, the underdog candidate ...*

TAKE THE NEXT STEP

What if writer's block was a word game, where you had to put words into blocks of pre-set patterns to form a shape poem?

Use this example to try it on your own.

DECEMBERSERK

Finish the story.

There is no one more

berserk than _____

on Christmas Eve.

TAKE THE NEXT STEP

Shop through your December memories and make a list of six.

Use these to prompt further writings.

All the Angles

Use the starters provided and the shapes as you like.

He played all the angles …

She knew all the angles …

TAKE THE NEXT STEP

If you have a new angle on an issue, write an op-ed piece and send it to your local paper. If it's printed, it's a good way to get a bit of local fame and can also be a stepping-stone to other writing opportunities. Jot down some op-ed ideas now.

LOOK AROUND YOU. NOTICE ALL
THE GOLD THINGS. WRITE DOWN
THE FIRST SIX YOU SEE:

USE ALL SIX IN A PIECE. START WITH:
SOMETIMES THE DULLEST ...

GOLD MOLD

TAKE THE NEXT STEP

Even the dullest of writing days can be brightened with a laugh. Try this:
Take off your shoes and socks. Put a pen/pencil between the two toes of
your choice. Now sign your name. Don't be afraid to enjoy yourself ... or
else it's time to get a new hobby!

Boys Will Be Boys

Finish the story. Start with: *At an early age, the little boy discovered …*

TAKE THE NEXT STEP

Do you think you might possess some creative talents you have yet to discover? List some possibilities. Commit to exploring one of these in the next three months. What first step will you take toward this commitment?

Comfort Foods

Ice Cream   Macaroni and Cheese   Mashed Potatoes

Cream of Wheat   Chicken Noodle Soup

Use all of these foods in a piece that begins:
He always looked uncomfortable …

TAKE THE NEXT STEP

No need to feel uncomfortable if you're not a good speller. To learn that alright and alot are not words, remember: It's all right to use your dictionary (or spell checker) a lot. For easy referral, list correct versions of some of your spelling challenges on a sheet in your writing area.

Winter of My Disc and Tent

Finish the story...

After I finished recording my _____ . I hit the road to sell it. With barely enough _____ to make ends meet, I decided to camp in my old scouting _____ . My first stop, on February 1st, was Des Moines, _____ . I met a lovely _____ who ...

...
_____
_____
_____
_____
_____
_____
_____
_____
_____
_____
_____

_____
_____
_____
_____
_____
_____

TAKE THE NEXT STEP

Brainstorm some names as if you were starting a writing business or a business that incorporates your writing talents. Make sure it describes who you are and what you do.

IDIOMS DELIGHT 4

Start with the idiom:
He'll never set the world on fire.

Use the idiomatic expression
Fish or cut bait in your conclusion.

TAKE THE NEXT STEP

If the dictionary police asked you to help define some new words, what definition would you supply for KWIT?

Do you realize you just redefined the word QUIT? Remember: Words are only as powerful as you make them.

ME TIMES THIRTY-THREE

Use the word *me* thirty-three times in this piece. As you write each *me*, number it so you can keep track. The first *me* is provided for you! Start with: *She handed me the …*

TAKE THE NEXT STEP

Speaking of you … grade your writing work habits here. (A-F)

[ ] completes projects on time   [ ] keeps a tidy area   [ ] asks for help

[ ] mentors others   [ ] keeps eye on goals   [ ] organized

[ ] motivated to write   [ ] does paperwork   [ ] inquisitive

ZZZZZZZZZZZZZZZZZZZ

Finish the story.

Start with:
*Now I recall,
that was the day
I overslept …*

TAKE THE NEXT STEP

What writing task could you accomplish if you set your alarm fifteen minutes earlier just for tomorrow?

Do it. You'll feel great the rest of the day. What could you accomplish if you did this the day after tomorrow, too?

DAY**344**

At-eeeeeeeeeee-tude

Finish the story. Start with: *Born on the wrong side of the tracks, she was a tough …*

TAKE THE NEXT STEP

With whom do you feel most comfortable being your writer-self? Why? With whom do you feel most uncomfortable being your writer-self? Why? Do something to change this.

DAY**345**

Come up with five creative
uses for an ashtray (other than
obvious container uses):

1.

2.

3.

4.

5.

Ashes to Ashes

Creatively incorporate these
five "uses" in a piece starting with:
The cold was unbearable …

TAKE THE NEXT STEP

List two negative things you say to your writer-self. Cut
them out with scissors. Put them in an ashtray. Burn them.
Replace them with positive words.

DAY**346**

Elements, Dear Watson

Write four short shorts about the elements. Be as metaphorical as you like. Use the starters provided.

The earth sounds …

The wind looks …

The rain tastes …

The fire smells …

TAKE THE NEXT STEP

One more. The act of writing feels …

Walk in the Park - Two

→ You are out walking. Two joggers pass you. You overhear a tiny tidbit of their conversation: "... And then I got to shake hands with Benjamin Franklin..." You are certain this is what you heard. Imagine on paper what it is they were talking about. (or continue their conversation in dialogue format.)

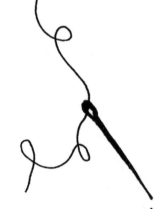

TAKE THE NEXT STEP

Use "a stitch in time saves nine" to remember that when referring to numbers, you spell out zero through nine. Use figures for 10 and above. Figures are also used for ages, address numbers, measurements. Go back through this book and make corrections. For fun, count the number of changes you have to make.

Adjacent Adjectives

Use the adjacent adjectives on the page as you get to them. Start with, *I kissed him* ...

red hot

smooth dark

cold wet

soft fuzzy

TAKE THE NEXT STEP

Comparing yourself to others is very detrimental to your creativity. Next time you find yourself doing this, generate a list of adjectives. Every time one describes you, write it down. At the end of ten minutes, combine the adjectives to describe yourself. It will be different every time. *Try it now.*

Snow Day

Finish the story. Start with:

The worst snow storm was the winter ...

TAKE THE NEXT STEP

One way to develop your powers of observation is to not listen to the "experts." For example, observe the sky, the outdoors, the current weather. Describe it, perhaps forecast it, and then listen to the weather person. Try it and see how different or accurate you are.

PEEPHOLE 3

You look
through the peephole of your
front door and see Santa Claus.
Play out the story. Start with: It's not
always easy to determine the sex of …

TAKE THE NEXT STEP

How does sticking to the exercises in this
book fit into the 'big picture' of your life?

Connect these prefixes, roots, and suffixes as you like to come up with four made up words:

Prefix	Root	Suffix	Your Made-up Words
mal	money	licious	1.
free	pure	MENT	2.
bi	layer	ling	3.
NON	TREE	ism	4.

USE ALL FOUR IN THIS STORY. START WITH:

I get such a kick out of ...

TAKE THE NEXT STEP

When you link money with writing practice, does it give you an extra-motivational kick? Or does it have the opposite effect? Why?

DAY**352**

X
marks the SPOT

Start with the supplied starter and then write anywhere and everywhere on the page, inside and outside the X. Use the spots as you get to them. They can be part of a drawing you use to illustrate your story, or bullet holes, or simply periods. Let your imagination guide you!

My ex-

TAKE THE NEXT STEP

If you were to closely EXamine the EXpectations you have for yourself as a writer, would you say they propel you forward or stop you in your tracks—or somewhere in the middle? EXplain.

DAY**353**

Pain &
Pleasure

Finish the story. When it comes to _____ there's a fine line between pain and pleasure for me.

TAKE THE NEXT STEP

Acrobats have a safety net. Writers have a network of support. Who in your network causes more pain than pleasure? What can you do to eliminate this obstacle? What can you do to further build your network to strengthen your writing?

PETITE PARAGRAPHS
FOUR

Here is a chance to write short paragraphs of memory snippets. Use the starters provided.

I remember tormenting …

I remember walking …

I remember diving …

I remember begging …

I remember bragging …

I remember dividing …

TAKE THE NEXT STEP

When in need of a quick writing exercise, you can always start with *I remember, I want, I seem,* or *I feel*. Come up with some others to use in the future.

SENSORY OVERLOAD

WRITE DOWN THE FOLLOWING:

Something you see at an executive conference:_____

A clothing texture you like:_____

A smell from the city:_____

A sound associated with a farm:_____

A taste reminiscent of your childhood:_____

Use all five items in your writing. Start with: *The cathedral bell …*

TAKE THE NEXT STEP

Every July 4th, the Liberty Bell is symbolically rung. It's too cracked to really strike. Whenever I want to congratulate myself but my situation restricts me from doing so, I make a fist with my left hand and lift it quickly upward once. No one notices and I feel great. What physical gesture can you come up with to silently acknowledge yourself?

DAY**356**

I FAILED JAIL

USE THE WORDS AS YOU COME TO THEM. START WITH: WHEN I OPENED MY EYES

AND REALIZED I WAS IN JAIL, I_____

_____JAIL_____FAIL____

_____BAIL_____GAIL_____

_____HAIL_____MAIL_____

_____NAIL_____

_____PAIL_____RAIL_____

_____SAIL_____

_____TAIL_____FAIL_____

_____JAIL_____.

TAKE THE NEXT STEP

Is there an issue or a person for whom you'd go to jail? Who? What? Why? Fuel your writing with this type of emotion and it will always be powerful to the reader.

GRAY
matter

Finish the story.

Start with: *It's the gray areas that ...*

_____
_____
_____
_____
_____
_____
_____
_____
_____
_____
_____
_____
_____
_____

TAKE THE NEXT STEP

If there was a writing scholarship in your honor, what would it be called? Who would be eligible? How often would it be given out? What would the criteria be? When and where would it be given? Would you be anonymous?

Snapshots

Four

Photos are a great way to capture memories. But we don't always have a camera with us. Write quick "word snapshots" as substitutes for the following topics. Try to capture colors, textures, and expressions. Use your own life story … or make them up!

Learning To Ride a Bicycle:

A New Car:

In a Costume:

A Contagious Smile:

TAKE THE NEXT STEP

Picture your writing-self as a house. What ideas would you keep in each of these rooms?

Powder room
Master bedroom
Attic
Spare bedroom

Xmas on Mars

Write six words or phrases pertaining to Christmas here:

_____ _____ _____
_____ _____ _____

Use all six in a story.
Start with: *Back when I was six and Mars was ...*

TAKE THE NEXT STEP

You may not get to go on a mission to Mars. But you can
have a personal writing mission statement. Write one.
(Cover principles, plans, who you are, foundations, etc.)
Use it when you tell others about your writing.

WHAT THE HECK?

Finish the story.

START WITH: **"WHAT THE HECK AM I SUPPOSED TO DO WITH THIS?"** SHE ...

TAKE THE NEXT STEP

"Do or do not. There is no try." *~ Yoda*

Try to pick up this book. Notice that you are either picking it up or not picking it up. There is no middle ground. There is no such thing as try. Eliminate try from your vocabulary. Don't say, "I'm trying to write a screenplay." Say, "I am writing a screenplay." Hear how much better it sounds?

JOY TO THE WORLD

Fill the page. Start with: She found joy in the most …

TAKE THE NEXT STEP

"Fear is that little darkroom where negatives are developed."
– Michael Pritchard

Where are the places where you enjoy your creative joys? Be spontaneous, visit one of these today. If you can't physically go, then go there in your imagination.

Faith Arthur Grant

Jason Kelly

Autograph

Write about getting an autograph from a famous person
whom you've idolized for a very long time. Use these
five words in your story: fly swatter, scale, rye bread,
law, ebony. Start with: I always carry a pen with me,
except for the time ...

TAKE THE NEXT STEP

TV shows have spin-offs, movies have sequels. What are some current or complete projects you can turn into sidebars or articles? How can you spin-off one of the exercises in this book and turn it into an article or an op-ed?

Ohio
TAG-3
HAMILTON 6-08

In Pennsylvania, most license plates are three letters and four numbers. Example: BMN 1958. For this exercise use the three letters as the first letters of the three beginning words in your story. Example: Because Most Nice. Use the four digit number, 1958, somewhere in your story. Example: A study says that nice people are 1,958 times more likely to say yes.

Start here:

B_____ M_____ N_____

_____

_____

_____

_____

_____

_____

_____

_____

_____

TAKE THE NEXT STEP
Being too nice (taking on too much, or trying to be perfect, for example) may backfire and turn into self-sabotage. Be nice to yourself now and write all the things you want from others and from yourself that will help your writing. Then tell or ask someone for what you want. It's very freeing.

Utah

Florid

Alabama

53UIS3

Hawaii

Happy Endings 3

Use the last sentence at the bottom of the page to conclude your story.

(Last sentence from *A Meeting* by Guy de Maupassant.)

He never saw her again, nor did he ever discover whether she had told him a lie or was speaking the truth.

TAKE THE NEXT STEP

Go back through this book to make sure you weren't lying when you wanted to be laying.

	to lay	to lie
Infinitive	to lay	to lie
Present	lay(s)	lie(s)
Past	laid	lay
Past Participle	laid	lain
Present Participle	laying	lying

To lay means to put or place something down. *To lie* means to rest or recline.

Provide your own starter ...
and use the closing sentence
at the bottom of the page.

The End

... but there's nothing quite as
satisfying as finishing a book!

TAKE THE NEXT STEP

"Best advice on writing I've ever received:
Finish." *- Peter Mayle*

CONGRATULATIONS! How does it feel
to have completed this book and written
366 pages? How have you changed or
grown? *Keep up the momentum.*

THE DESIGN OF THIS BOOK

The designs on the pages of this book are the result of a huge collaborative effort. Thanks to all the design students, freelance designers, and staff designers who took part in this project. The designers thoroughly explored and expressed each writing prompt, resulting in pages that are stunning, intriguing, varied, and beautiful.

1 Claudean Wheeler	28 Michael Murphy,	55 Grace Ring
2 John Rizzo	Grace Ring	56 Lisa Kuhn
3 Ryan Stager	29 Claudean Wheeler	57 Lisa Kuhn
4 Rob Warner	30 Anne Gibble	58 Michael Murphy,
5 Grace Ring	31 Rob Warner	Grace Ring
6 Robin Richie,	32 Michelle Snyder	59 Rob Warner
Grace Ring	33 Claudean Wheeler	60 Lisa Kuhn
7 Rob Warner	34 Lisa Kuhn	61 Jazmine Atienza
8 Grace Ring	35 Claudean Wheeler	62 Kristy Wunderlich
9 Claudean Wheeler	36 Rob Warner	63 Tari Clidence
10 Kelly Kofron	37 Anne Gibble	64 Rob Warner
11 Grace Ring	38 Amy Schell, Grace Ring	65 Cassandra Bell
12 Rob Warner	39 Rob Warner	66 Claudean Wheeler
13 Anne Gibble	40 Rob Warner	67 Rob Warner
14 Tricia Bateman	41 Lisa Kuhn	68 Amy Schell, Grace Ring
15 Lisa Kuhn	42 Rob Warner	69 Anne Gibble
16 Claudean Wheeler	43 Grace Ring	70 Claudean Wheeler
17 Claudean Wheeler	44 Lisa Kuhn	71 Erica Hansen
18 Claudean Wheeler	45 Claudean Wheeler	72 Rob Warner
19 Rob Warner	46 Alice Pope, Grace Ring	73 Lisa Kuhn
20 Claudean Wheeler	47 Grace Ring	74 Ryan Stager
21 LeAnne Wagner	48 Claudean Wheeler	75 Michael Murphy,
22 Rob Warner	49 Lisa Kuhn	Grace Ring
23 Ryan Stager	50 Rob Warner	76 Jen Rust
24 Lisa Barlow	51 Lisa Kuhn	77 Rob Warner
25 Rob Warner	52 Ryan Stager	78 Rob Warner
26 Beth Alexander Willman	53 Karla Baker	79 Claudean Wheeler
27 Lisa Kuhn	54 Derrick Schultz	80 Lisa Kuhn

81 Beth Alexander Willman
82 Rob Warner
83 Lisa Kuhn
84 Lisa Kuhn, Grace Ring
85 Neal Miles
86 Robin Richie,
   Grace Ring
87 Marissa Bowers
88 Kelly Kofron
89 Karla Baker
90 Vina Parel Ayers
91 Lisa Kuhn
92 John Rizzo
93 Lisa Kuhn
94 Rob Warner
95 Claudean Wheeler
96 Lila Szagun
97 Kelly Kofron
98 Rob Warner
99 Lisa Barlow
100 Claudean Wheeler
101 Lisa Kuhn
102 Claudean Wheeler
103 Rob Warner
104 Claudean Wheeler
105 Cassandra Bell
106 Lisa Kuhn
107 Kelly Kofron
108 Claudean Wheeler
109 Kara Beisner
110 Rob Warner
111 Derrick Schultz
112 Grace Ring
113 Claudean Wheeler
114 Alice Pope, Grace Ring
115 Rob Warner
116 Lisa Kuhn
117 Ryan Stager
118 Dru Sidle
119 Grace Ring
120 Claudean Wheeler
121 Claudean Wheeler
122 Brendan Bruce
123 Anne Gibble
124 Ryan Stager
125 Karla Baker
126 Lisa Kuhn
127 Rob Warner
128 Lisa Kuhn
129 Rob Warner

130 Beth Alexander Willman
131 Lisa Kuhn
132 Claudean Wheeler
133 Claudean Wheeler
134 Lisa Kuhn
135 Lisa Kuhn
136 Rob Warner
137 Grace Ring
138 Claudean Wheeler
139 Rob Warner
140 Lisa Kuhn
141 Erica Hansen
142 Rob Warner
143 Claudean Wheeler
144 Rob Warner
145 Rob Warner
146 Lisa Kuhn
147 Anne Gibble
148 Lisa Kuhn
149 Ryan Stager
150 Lisa Kuhn
151 Alice Pope,
    Claudean Wheeler
152 Jazmine Atienza
153 Anne Gibble
154 Rob Warner
155 Kelly Kofron
156 Rob Warner
157 John Rizzo
158 Lisa Kuhn
159 Lisa Kuhn
160 Grace Ring
161 Claudean Wheeler
162 Claudean Wheeler
163 Jason Bradley
164 Claudean Wheeler
165 Lisa Barlow
166 Lisa Kuhn
167 Ryan Stager
168 Rob Warner
169 Claudean Wheeler
170 Heidi Bartlett
171 Marissa Bowers
172 Rob Warner
173 Lisa Kuhn
174 Lisa Kuhn
175 Rob Warner
176 Lisa Kuhn
177 John Rizzo
178 Rob Warner

179 Beth Alexander Willman
180 Lisa Kuhn
181 Claudean Wheeler
182 Rob Warner
183 Lisa Kuhn
184 Lisa Kuhn
185 Lisa Kuhn
186 Beth Toner
187 Rob Warner
188 Grace Ring
189 LeAnne Wagner
190 Lisa Kuhn
191 Kara Beisner
192 Rob Warner
193 Vina Parel Ayers
194 Suzanne Lucas,
    Grace Ring
195 Rob Warner
196 Claudean Wheeler
197 Dru Sidle
198 Ryan Stager
199 Kelly Nickell,
    Grace Ring
200 Claudean Wheeler
201 Rob Warner
202 Kelly Kofron
203 Lisa Kuhn
204 Rob Warner
205 Michelle Ruberg,
    Grace Ring
206 Tricia Bateman
207 Rob Warner
208 Karla Baker
209 Claudean Wheeler
210 Ryan Stager
211 Lisa Kuhn
212 Lisa Kuhn,
    Claudean Wheeler
213 Rob Warner
215 Lisa Kuhn
216 Kristen Kozelouzek
217 Rob Warner
218 Rob Warner
219 Lisa Kuhn
220 Ryan Stager
221 Claudean Wheeler
222 Anne Gibble
223 Lisa Kuhn
224 Phil Sexton,
    Grace Ring

225 Lisa Kuhn
226 Alice Pope,
    Claudean Wheeler
227 Ryan Stager
228 Lisa Kuhn
229 Carrie Brunk
230 Claudean Wheeler
231 Lisa Kuhn
232 Amy Schell, Grace Ring
233 Rob Warner
234 Rob Warner
235 Marissa Bowers
236 Lisa Kuhn
237 Rob Warner
238 Kelly Kofron
239 Ryan Stager
240 Lisa Kuhn
241 Ryan Stager
242 John Rizzo
243 Lisa Kuhn
244 Lisa Kuhn
245 Claudean Wheeler
246 Suzanne Lucas,
    Claudean Wheeler
247 Ryan Stager
248 Cassandra Bell
249 Anne Gibble
250 Ryan Stager
251 Lisa Kuhn
252 Ryan Stager
253 Michelle Ruberg,
    Grace Ring
254 Erica Hansen
255 Tari Clidence
256 Ryan Stager
257 Rebecca Cook
258 Claudean Wheeler
259 Derrick Schultz
260 Rob Warner
261 Melissa Weber
262 Lisa Kuhn
263 Erica Hansen
264 Ryan Stager
265 Ryan Stager
266 Ryan Stager
267 Lisa Kuhn
268 Lisa Kuhn
269 Ryan Stager
270 Neal Miles
271 Ryan Stager

272 Lisa Kuhn
273 John Rizzo
274 Beth Alexander Willman
275 Rob Warner
276 Lisa Kuhn
277 Rob Warner
278 Kristy Wunderlich
279 Lisa Kuhn
280 Jen Brenner
281 Rob Warner
282 Rob Warner
283 Lisa Kuhn
284 Lisa Kuhn
285 Phil Sexton,
    Grace Ring
286 Rob Warner
287 Lisa Kuhn
288 John Rizzo
289 Lisa Kuhn
290 Lisa Kuhn
291 Rob Warner
292 John Rizzo
293 Rob Warner
294 Lisa Kuhn
295 Ryan Stager
296 Claudean Wheeler
297 Lisa Kuhn
298 Lisa Kuhn
299 Claudean Wheeler
300 Rob Warner
301 Karla Baker
302 Erica Hansen
303 Lisa Kuhn
304 Rob Warner
305 Erica Hansen
306 Rob Warner
307 Lisa Kuhn
308 Heidi Bartlett
309 Lisa Kuhn
310 Rob Warner
311 Marissa Bowers
312 Rob Warner
313 Claudean Wheeler
314 Lisa Kuhn
315 Rob Warner
316 Lisa Kuhn
317 Rob Warner
318 John Rizzo
319 Rob Warner
320 Erica Hansen

321 Lisa Kuhn
322 Rob Warner
323 Carrie Brunk
324 Rob Warner
325 Lisa Kuhn
326 Lisa Kuhn
327 Rob Warner
328 LeAnne Wagner
329 Lisa Kuhn
330 Rob Warner
331 Grace Ring
332 Rob Warner
333 Lisa Kuhn
334 Cassandra Bell
335 Rob Warner
336 Jason Bradley
337 Rob Warner
338 Lisa Kuhn
339 Rob Warner
340 Lisa Kuhn
341 Dru Sidle
342 Ryan Stager
343 John Rizzo
344 Rob Warner
345 Rob Warner
346 Kristy Wunderlich
347 Michelle Stevenson
348 Jen Brenner
349 Rob Warner
350 Grace Ring
351 Lisa Kuhn
352 Kevin Witter
353 Claudean Wheeler
354 Rob Warner
355 Karla Baker
356 Claudean Wheeler
357 Lisa Kuhn
358 Erica Hansen
359 Rob Warner
360 Rob Warner
361 Karla Baker
362 Rob Warner
363 Lisa Kuhn
364 Lisa Kuhn
365 Rob Warner
366 Lisa Kuhn

STORY SPINNER

Story Spinner is a handheld creative writing wheel that generates millions of writing ideas and topics so you never get stuck. It's a low-tech item that produces high-caliber results, time after time, no matter where you are.

Story Spinner is perfect for:

TEACHERS: An instant creative writing lesson plan.

WRITERS, ARTISTS, ACTORS: Never be blocked again.

PARENTS: Encourage your kids' creativity.

STUDENTS: Finally, help with writing assignments.

GIFTS: For that creative person in your life ... or yourself!!!

Here's an example of a prompt generated by the story spinner.

1. The purple wheel gives you a phrase to start your story. Yours is: "It was 1970"

2. The black wheel gives you a setting to locate your story. Yours is: "in the woods"

3. The red wheel gives you a word you must include in your story. Yours is: "hypnotist"

4. Now, set a timer for ten minutes, start with "It was 1970" and write, draw, act or tell your story. Don't forget to set it "in the woods" and use the word "hypnotist"!

To buy your very own Story Spinner (just $9.99 plus $1.00 s/h per Spinner in the U.S.) so you can have more of these fun creative writing exercises wherever you go, send check or money order to Story Spinner, P.O. Box 810, Ardmore, PA 19003. For more information go to www.bonnieneubauer.com and click on the Story Spinner link or send an e-mail to spinner@bonnieneubauer.com or call 610-446-7441.

BOOKS OF INTEREST

More great ideas from Writer's Digest Books!

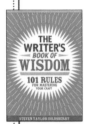

THE WRITER'S BOOK OF WISDOM
By Steven Taylor Goldsberry

The Writer's Book of Wisdom contains 101 of the best rules you'll ever want to follow to become a better writer. Packed with lessons and inspiration, each page of this cozy, inviting book contains condensed, concise instruction framed by splashes of color on each snappily designed page. Read through a lesson, think it through, and still have time to write!
ISBN 1-58297-292-3, pob, 224 pages, #10940

PAGE AFTER PAGE
by Heather Sellers

Treat yourself to this highly original, charmingly quirky, and dazzling piece of exceptional work. Reminiscent of *Bird by Bird* by Anne Lamott, *Page After Page* will help you establish a productive, happy writing life and achieve your writing goals.
ISBN 1-58297-312-1, hc, 240 pages, #10948

ROBERT'S RULES OF WRITING
by Robert Masello

This book delivers 101 of the most original, uninhibited techniques designed to improve the work of fiction writers, freelancers, memoirists, and screenwriters. When tried-and-true instruction just keeps you stuck in a writing rut, it's time to break out *Robert's Rules of Writing*. Transform your writing life and get published today!
ISBN 1-58297-326-1, pb, 224 pages, #10962

These and other fine books from Writer's Digest are available at your local bookstore, online supplier or by calling 1-800-448-0915.